4

P. 64 - give Conclusion + re...

Bring in an ad. write write what it brings to mind

95

Ch 11
12
13
14
Read page 118

Asking
the
Right
Questions

100
90
80
85
50
─────
5

Ch 1 — 12
6 Issue in Con
Rea—
Ambigous word.
Value conflict
Flaws of statstcal rea—
Averg—
Are there eves u
Sig Quustion - mean
do study exercises on
Ch 12
read Instructions   141

· Ch 1 — 5
Page - 47.
Ch · 6 — 8
Skip - 7.

Asking
the
Right
Questions

A Guide to
Critical Thinking

SECOND EDITION

M. Neil Browne   Stuart M. Keeley

BOWLING GREEN STATE UNIVERSITY

Prentice-Hall, Inc.
Englewood Cliffs, N.J. 07632

Library of Congress Cataloging-in-Publication
Browne, M. Neil, 1944–
    Asking the right questions.
    Includes bibliographical references and index.
    1. Reading.   2. Criticism.   3. Thought and thinking.
I. Keeley, Stuart M., 1941–   . II. Title.
PN83.B785   1986   808   85-16915
ISBN 0-13-049438-0

Editorial/production supervision and interior design: Mark Stevens
Cover design: Wanda Lubelska
Manufacturing buyer: Harry P. Baisley

Printed in the United States of America

10 9 8 7 6 5 4 3 2 1

ISBN   0-13-049438-0   01

Prentice-Hall International (UK) Limited, *London*
Prentice-Hall of Australia Pty. Limited, *Sydney*
Editora Prentice-Hall do Brasil, Ltda., *Rio de Janeiro*
Prentice-Hall Canada Inc., *Toronto*
Prentice-Hall Hispanoamericana, S.A., *Mexico*
Prentice-Hall of India Private Limited, *New Delhi*
Prentice-Hall of Japan, Inc., *Tokyo*
Prentice-Hall of Southeast Asia Pte. Ltd., *Singapore*
Whitehall Books Limited, *Wellington, New Zealand*

To my grandparents, Gladys and Hoy,
    for their legacy of independence and love;
To Gretchen and Shannon,
    with the hope the legacy will be maintained.

M. N. B.

To Barb and the kids for their patience.

S. M. K.

Contents

Preface

This second edition of *Asking the Right Questions* results from the enthusiastic support of our readers. Following their advice, we have built on the strengths of the first edition. This edition continues our emphasis on values and moral reasoning as an integral part of critical thinking. We have retained a format that is explicitly logical, readable, and succinct. Where appropriate, we have revised and updated practice exercises and examples, and in particular have attempted to improve several of the sample answers to the practice exercises where our readers had noted possible confusion.

Three improvements in this edition are noteworthy. Many who have used the first edition urged us to include brief sections on the impact of critical thinking skills on expository writing. While we wanted to be responsive to this suggestion, we did not want to significantly increase the text's length. Hence, at the ends of several chapters we have included brief suggestions about the usefulness of particular critical-thinking skills for clear writing, pointing out to the student the relationship among critical thinking, critical reading, and clear written communication.

A second major improvement has been the addition of longer arguments for students to analyze. While we have retained the brevity of most of the practice exercises, we have also included several lengthier essays to give students the opportunity to evaluate more complex arguments. This improvement stemmed from the almost universal request of our reviewers that we include arguments of varying length.

A third addition is the inclusion in the final chapter of a long example illustrating the systematic use of critical-thinking skills in expository writing.

We were motivated to write the first edition of this book by a variety of personal experiences and observations. First, we were dismayed at the degree to which students and acquaintances showed an increasing dependence on "experts"—textbook writers, teachers, lawyers, politicians, journalists, and TV commentators. As the complexity of the world seems to grow at an accelerating rate, there is a greater tendency to become passive absorbers of information, uncritically accepting what is seen and heard. We became concerned that too many of us are not actively participating in making personal choices about what to accept and what to reject.

Second, our experience in teaching critical-thinking skills to our students over a number of years convinced us that when individuals with diverse abilities are taught these skills in a simplified format, they can learn to apply them successfully in diverse situations. In the process they develop great confidence in their ability to make rational choices about certain social issues, even those with which they have formerly had little experience.

A third motivating factor was our inability to find a book with which to teach the skills we wanted students to learn. We did not want a philosophy text, but rather a book that, while informal in nature, would outline basic critical-reading skills explicitly, concisely, and simply. We did not find such a book.

Thus, we set out to write a text that would do a number of things that other books had failed to do. The text that resulted attempts to develop an integrated series of question-asking skills which can be applied to a wide variety of reading material, from textbooks to magazine essays. These skills are discussed in an informal style. (We have written to a general audience, not to any specialized group.)

We provide many opportunities for the readers to apply their skills and to receive immediate feedback following the practice application. The book is replete with examples of writing devoted to controversial contemporary topics. The breadth of topics introduces the average reader to writings on numerous controversies with which he or she may have little familiarity. The book is coherently organized, in that critical questions are discussed sequentially as the reader progresses from asking questions to making decisions. In addition, it integrates cognitive and value dimensions—a very important aspect of critical reading and personal decision making.

Who would find *Asking the Right Questions* especially beneficial? Because of our teaching experiences with readers representing many different levels of ability, we have difficulty envisioning any academic course or program for which this book would not be useful. In fact, the first edition has been used in law, English, pharmacy, philosophy, education, psychology, sociology, religion, and social science courses.

A few uses for the book seem especially appropriate. Teachers in general education programs may want to begin their courses by assigning it as a coherent response to their students' requests to explain what is expected of them. English courses that emphasize expository writing could use this text both as a format for evaluating arguments prior to constructing an essay and as a checklist of problems that the writer should attempt to avoid as he or she writes. Courses training prospective teachers should find the book especially functional because it makes explicit much that teachers will want to encourage in their students. Courses in study-skill development may be enriched by supplementing their current content with our step-by-step description of the process of critical reading and thinking. The text can also be used as the central focus of courses designed specifically to teach critical reading and thinking skills.

While *Asking the Right Questions* stems primarily from our classroom experiences, it is written so that it can guide the reading habits of almost anyone. The skills that it seeks to develop are those that any critical reader needs to possess if reading is to serve as a basis for rational decisions. The critical questions stressed in the book can enliven anyone's reading, regardless of the extent of his or her formal education.

This second edition is the product of suggestions from many thoughtful readers. Especially helpful have been our students and colleagues at Bowling Green State University. While we have received helpful comments from a large number of readers, several have been unusually incisive in their suggestions. In appreciation for their help, we want to thank David Bernstein, Robert Boenig, Terrence Doyle, Kathleen Hart, Carol Hunts, Lynne Kellermann, Tom Klein, Nancy Kubasek, and Walter Minot. This second edition has profited greatly from our conversations with Paul Haas and Jim Litwin, as did the first edition. In association with these dedicated teachers, we have tried to encourage the habit of asking critical questions.

I

The Benefit of
Asking
the Right Questions

Introduction

Each of us is bombarded with information. Every day we encounter new facts and opinions. In textbooks, newspapers, and magazines, writers present ideas they want us to accept. One social scientist tells us violence on television is bad for our children; another tells us it does no harm. One economist argues for reducing taxes to stem inflation; another argues that we should increase interest rates. One educational critic recommends eliminating the "frills," such as foreign language and physical education requirements; another recommends we expand such "necessities." In all areas of knowledge there are issues about which experts in those fields disagree. You as a reader have the tough job of deciding which authority to believe. Whether you are reading a nursing journal, a critique of a poem, a textbook, or even the sports page, you will be faced with the problem of deciding which conclusions to accept, which to reject, and which to withhold judgment on.

As a reader you must make a choice about how you will react to what you read. One alternative is to accept passively what is written, which automatically results in your making the writer's opinion your own. A more active alternative consists of asking questions of yourself in an effort to reach a personal decision about the worth of what you have read. This book is written for those who prefer the second alternative.

Reading critically—that is, reacting to what you read through systematic evaluation—requires a special set of skills. These skills basically consist of the ability to ask and answer a series of critical questions. These questions are useful whenever you want to react to what you are reading. This book presents these questions and systematically guides you in using them, in an easy, understandable way.

These skills will be helpful to you both as a student and as a citizen. As a student, they should be especially useful whenever you are asked to

1. react critically to an essay or to evidence presented in a textbook,
2. form an argument,
3. write an essay based on a reading assignment,
4. participate in class.

As a citizen, they should be especially helpful in shaping your voting behavior and your purchasing decisions, and improving your self-confidence by increasing your feelings of intellectual independence.

The Filter and the Sponge: Alternative Thinking Styles

One approach to reading is similar to the way in which a sponge reacts to water: by *absorbing*. This commonly used approach has some clear advantages.

First, the more information you absorb about the world, the more capable you are of understanding its complexities. Knowledge you have acquired provides a foundation for more complicated thinking later. For instance, it would be very difficult to judge the value of a sociological theory before you had absorbed a core of knowledge about sociology.

A second advantage of the sponge approach is that it is relatively passive. Rather than requiring strenuous mental effort, it tends to be rather quick and easy, especially when the material is presented in a clear and interesting fashion. The primary mental effort is concentration and memory.

While absorbing information provides a productive start toward becoming a thoughtful person, the sponge approach has a serious disadvantage: It provides no method for deciding which information and opinions to believe and which to reject. If a reader relied on the sponge approach all the time, she would believe whatever she read *last*.

We think you would rather choose for yourself what to absorb and what to ignore. To make this choice, you must read with a special attitude— a question-asking attitude. Such a thinking style requires active participation. The writer is trying to speak to you, and you should try to talk back to him, even though he is not present. We call this interactional approach the *filter approach*. The term *filter* is used to emphasize the actions of the reader in separating out "impurities," in seeking to find the essential elements, and ultimately, in determining the worth of the elements. The emphasis of this approach is on asking questions and thinking about material. The sponge approach emphasizes knowledge acquisition; the filter approach stresses the process of active interaction with knowledge. Thus, the two approaches often complement each other.

Let us more closely examine how the two approaches lead to different behavior. What does the individual who takes the sponge approach do when he reads material? He reads sentences carefully, trying to remember as much as he can. He may underline or highlight key words and sentences. He may take notes summarizing the major topics and major points. He checks his underlining or notes to be sure he is not forgetting anything important. His mission is to find out and understand what the author has to say.

What does the reader who takes the filter approach do? Like the person using the sponge approach, she approaches her reading with the hope that she will acquire new knowledge. Then the similarity ends. The filter approach requires that the reader ask herself a number of questions, to clarify logical steps in the material and help identify important omissions. The reader who uses the filter approach frequently questions why the author makes various claims. She writes notes to herself in the margins indicating problems with the reasoning. She continually interacts with the material. Her intent is to critically evaluate the material and formulate personal conclusions based on the evaluation.

An Example of the Filter Approach in Action

One topic we all get excited about is the size of our taxes. Consequently, there is always someone suggesting that our taxes are too high. Let's look together at one hypothetical proposal for a tax cut. Try to decide whether the argument is convincing.

> Every dollar that we pay in taxes is a dollar that we cannot spend on food, clothing, and shelter. At a time when newspapers are full of debate about the number of hungry and homeless in our country, it is strange indeed that we willingly give the government 30 percent of all our earnings. This tax money could be used by the hungry and homeless to satisfy their needs. Instead, what little income they have is drained away by the taxing authorities.
>
> When tax cuts have occurred in our history, prosperity soon followed. The logic of that result is clear. The more money you keep, the more you will spend. When you spend money, you create jobs and income. Reduce our taxes and you will reduce our unemployment rate.

If you apply the sponge approach to the passage, you probably would try to remember the reasons why you should favor a tax cut and perhaps try to understand them. If so, you will have absorbed some knowledge. However, are you sure that you should find those reasons convincing? You cannot evaluate them until you have used the filter approach—that is, until you have asked the right questions.

By asking the right questions, you would discover a number of possible weaknesses in the proposal for a tax cut. For instance, you might be concerned about all of the following:

1. Does $1 million used to create jobs in the private sector create *exactly* the same number of jobs as would be created by a $1 million expenditure by government?
2. Are there factors that caused other tax cuts to be successful that are different now?
3. Are there alternative ways to create economic growth that would cause less harm?
4. What would we lose as a result of tax cuts?

If you want to ask these kinds of questions, this book is especially for you. Its primary purpose is to help you know when and how to ask questions that will enable you to decide what to believe.

The most important characteristic of the filter approach is *interactive involvement*—a dialogue between the writer and the reader.

Clearly, there are times when the sponge approach is appropriate. Most of you have used it regularly and have acquired some level of success with it. It is much less likely that you are in the habit of employing the filter approach—in part, simply because you have not had the filters. This book will not only help you develop these filters, but will also provide frequent opportunities for practicing their use.

Active Filtering: Asking Critical Questions

It would be nice if what other people were really saying was always obvious, if all their essential thoughts were clearly labeled for us, and if the writer never made an error in his or her reasoning. If this were the case, we could read passively and let others do our thinking for us. However, the true state of affairs is quite the opposite. A writer's reasoning is often not obvious. Important elements are often missing. Many elements that *are* present are unclear. Other elements that are present do not even belong there. Consequently, critical reading is a sorting process through which you must identify what makes sense and distinguish this clear thinking from the sloppy thinking that characterizes much of what you will read.

What's the point? The inadequacies in what someone says will not always leap out at you. You must be an *active* searcher. You can do this by *asking questions*. The best search strategy is a critical-questioning strategy.

Throughout the book we will be showing you why certain critical questions are so important to ask. A powerful advantage of these questions is that they permit you to ask searching questions even when you know very little about the topic being discussed. For example, you do not need to be an expert on child care to ask critical questions about the adequacy of day-care centers.

The Myth of the "Right Answer"

Our ability to find definite answers to questions often depends on the type of question that puzzles us. Scientific questions about the physical world are the most likely to have answers that reasonable people will accept, since the physical world is in certain ways more dependable or predictable than the social world. While the precise distance to the moon or the age of a newly discovered bone from an ancient civilization may not be absolutely certain, agreement about the dimensions of our physical environment is widespread. Thus, in the physical sciences, we frequently can arrive at "the right answer."

Questions about human behavior are different. The causes of human behavior are so complex and so difficult to apply high standards of evidence to that we frequently cannot do much more than form intelligent guesses about why or when certain behavior will occur. In addition, because many of us care a great deal about explanations and descriptions of human behavior, we prefer that explanations or descriptions of the rate of abortion, the frequency of unemployment, or the causes of child abuse be consistent with what we want to believe. Hence we bring our preferences to any discussion of those issues and resist arguments that are inconsistent with them.

Since human behavior is so controversial and complex, the best answers that we can find for many questions about our behavior will be probabilistic in nature, lacking a high degree of certainty. Even if we are aware of all the evidence available about the effects of running on our mental health, the nature of such questions about human behavior will prevent our discovering the *exact truth* about such effects.

Regardless of the type of question being asked, the issues that require your closest scrutiny are usually those about which "reasonable people" disagree. In fact, many issues are interesting exactly because there is strong disagreement about how to resolve them. Any controversy involves more than one position. Several positions may be supported with good reasons. Thus, when you engage in active reading, you should be seeking the position that seems most reasonable to you. There will seldom be a position on a social controversy about which you will be able to say, "This is clearly the right position on the issue." If this were the case, reasonable people would not be debating the issue. Our focus in this book will be on such social controversies.

Even though you will not necessarily arrive at the "right answer" to social controversies, this book is designed to give you the skills to develop your best and most reasonable answer, given the nature of the problem and the available information. Decisions usually must be made in the face of uncertainty. Often we will not have the time or the ability to discover many of the important facts about a decision we must make. For example, it is simply unwise to ask all the right questions when someone you love is complaining of sharp chest pains and wants you to transport him to the emergency room.

Questions First, Emotional Involvement Last

As you approach issues, you will often find yourself emotionally involved. It is only natural to have strong feelings about many issues. Successful, active learners try to recognize such feelings, however, and remain open to reasoned opinions. This is important because many of our own positions on issues are not especially reasonable ones; they are opinions given to us by others, and over many years we develop emotional attachments to them. Indeed, we frequently believe that we are being personally attacked when someone presents a conclusion contrary to our own. The danger of being emotionally involved in an issue prior to any active thought about it is that you may fail to consider potential good reasons for other positions—reasons which might be sufficient to change your mind on the issue if you would only listen to them.

Remember: Emotional involvement alone should not be the basis for accepting or rejecting a position. Ideally, emotional involvement should be most intense *after* reasoning has occurred. Thus, when you read, try to avoid letting emotional involvement cut you off from the reasoning of those with whom you initially disagree. A successful active learner is one who is willing to change his or her mind. If you are ever to change your mind, you must be as open as possible to ideas that strike you as weird or dangerous when you first encounter them.

Efficiency of Asking the Question, "Who Cares?"

Asking good questions is difficult but rewarding work. Some controversies will be much more important to you than others. When the consequences of a controversy for you and your community are minimal, you will want to spend less time and energy thinking critically about it than about more important controversies. For example, it makes sense to critically evaluate arguments for and against the building of nuclear power plants, because different positions on this issue lead to important consequences for society. It makes less sense to devote energy to evaluating whether or not blue is the favorite color of most corporation executives.

Your time is valuable. Before taking the time to critically evaluate an issue, ask the question, Who cares?

The Satisfaction of Using the Filter Approach

Doing is usually more fun than watching; doing well is more fun than simply doing. If you start using the interactive form of reading taught in this book, you can feel the same sense of pride in your reading that you normally get from successful participation.

Critical readers find it satisfying to know when to say no to an idea or opinion and to know why that response is appropriate. If you regularly use the filter approach, then anything that gets into your head will first have to pass through the filters you are using. Thus, you will be systematically testing all information and opinions. When an idea or belief *does* pass the tests developed here, it will make sense to agree with it—at least until new evidence appears.

Imagine how good you will feel if you know *why* you should ignore or accept a particular bit of advice. Frequently, those faced with an opinion different from their own respond by saying, "Oh, that's just your opinion." But the issue should not be whose opinion it is, but rather whether it is a good opinion. Armed with the critical questions discussed in this book, you can experience the satisfaction of knowing why certain advice is nonsense.

The sponge approach is often satisfying because it permits you to assimilate information. Though that is certainly productive, there is much more gratification in being a participant in a meaningful dialogue with the writer. Reading becomes much richer as you begin to see things that the author may have missed. As you question the correctness of her reasoning, you will start to go beyond what she wants you to believe. No one wants to be at the mercy of the last "expert" he meets. As you learn to select information and opinions systematically you will probably desire to read more and more, in a lifelong effort to decide which advice makes sense.

Effective Writing and Critical Reading

Many of the skills you will learn as you become a more critical reader will improve the quality of your writing. As you write it helps to be aware of the expectations careful readers will have. Since your objective is communication, many of the questions the reader will ask in evaluating your writing should serve as guides for your writing. For instance, several of the critical questions that we urge you to ask focus on problems you will want to avoid as you write.

While the emphasis in this book is on effective reading and thinking, the link to competent writing is so direct that it will be a theme throughout. Wherever appropriate, we will mention how the skill being encouraged is an aid to improved writing.

The Importance of Practice

Learning new critical-reading skills is a lot like learning new physical skills. You cannot learn simply by being told what to do or by watching others. You have to practice, and frequently the practice will be both rewarding and hard work. Our goal is to make your learning as simple as possible. However, acquiring the habit of critical reading will initially take a lot of practice.

The practice exercises at the end of each chapter are an important part of this text. Try to do the exercises and only then compare your answers with ours. Our answers are not necessarily the only correct ones, but they provide illustrations of how to apply the question-asking skills.

The Right Questions

To give you an initial sense of the skills that *Asking the Right Questions* will help you acquire, we will list the critical questions for you here. By the end of the book, you should know when and how to ask these questions productively.

1. What are the issue and the conclusion?
2. What are the reasons?
3. What words or phrases are ambiguous?
4. What are the value conflicts and assumptions?
5. What are the definitional and descriptive assumptions?
6. Are the samples representative and the measurements valid?
7. Are there flaws in the statistical reasoning?
8. Are there alternative causal explanations?
9. Are there any errors in reasoning?
10. What significant information is omitted?
11. What alternative conclusions are consistent with the strong reasons?
12. What are your value preferences in this controversy?

II

Recognizing the Writer's Organization

Words don't communicate until they are strung together in an *orderly sequence*. Thus, critical reading begins with a search for organization. Authors of articles and books usually follow a pattern as they write. You as a reader can evaluate, using the filter approach, only after you have first discovered the pattern or organization that the writer had in mind before you came into the picture. The very first step that active readers take is to search for organization. None of the more complex steps in the critical-reading process is particularly helpful until the organization is discovered.

Suppose you are reading the following selection:

(1) A recent survey of 3,000 young males found that 20 percent had lived with a woman for 6 months or more without being married. (2) Most of these 20 percent had done so with only one partner. (3) At the time of the interviews only 3 percent of the unmarried men were living with a woman. (4) Apparently, most American males are very traditional about the desirability of marriage.

What would you do with this passage when you read it? Would you underline certain key words? If so, which ones? Would you skim the four sentences because they don't look important? Would you evaluate it? Recognizing organization is the initial step in answering these important questions.

Active reading begins by recognizing organization.

Functions of Sentences and Paragraphs

Let's look more closely at the preceding passage. Each sentence has a function that links it to the surrounding sentences. Discovering these links is the first task in recognizing organization. Later in the book, we will help you evaluate how well each of these functions is performed; at this point, however, you may need more practice in simply identifying the function. Ask yourself what role each sentence in the passage is playing in relation to those that precede and follow it, and write out your ideas.

To check your mastery of the task, compare your answers with the ones we would have given:

SENTENCE 1 states the results of a survey concerning the extent to which couples live together.

SENTENCES 2 and 3 provide an additional finding which clarifies the evidence in sentence (1).

SENTENCE 4 presents the author's conclusion based on the three previous sentences.

Critical thinking requires us to look closely at *how well* the four sentences perform these various functions. However, that step must be postponed until we have examined other elements of structure which will be discussed in the next two chapters.

Just as sentences have a function, so do paragraphs. As you read, it is a good idea to *jot down in the margin* your ideas about the function of particular paragraphs. Writing a brief note to yourself that indicates what each paragraph does in relation to the surrounding ones provides a sound basis for critical reading. It is frequently helpful to *group paragraphs* together, since authors will often use several paragraphs to fulfill a single function. Marginal notations give you a quick overview of the writer's organization.

What are some of the major functions that sentences and paragraphs fulfill? Subsequent chapters of the book will go into detail about some of these functions; at this point we want to mention just a few of the organizational functions to look for as you read. Among the more important roles played by sentences and paragraphs are the following:

1. background information,
2. statement of the controversy,
3. definitions,
4. examples of the problem,
5. research methodology,
6. evidence,
7. reason,
8. counterargument,
9. summary,
10. conclusion.

Let's look at another example of a possible reading assignment.

(1) Central to many arguments involving advertising's varied economic *argumentative*
effects and influences is the question of whether advertising is related
to product quality. (2) Are heavily advertised brands better than other
brands in the same product class? (3) Is advertising a sign of higher
product quality?

(4) The issue discussed herein is not whether the higher price is worth
the information advertising provides the consumer, but rather whether
extensive advertising is positively associated with highly ranked prod- *Thesis*
ucts as defined by some objective standards. (5) In this study we adopted
the product ratings of two recognized, independent consumer product *research*
testing agencies (*Consumer Reports* and *Consumer Research Magazine*) as
our objective standards of quality.

(6) Though 21.3 percent of the heavily advertised brands received rec- *research*
ommended ratings, so did 18.2 percent of the less-heavily advertised
brands. (7) Do heavily advertised products tend to be of higher quality?
(8) On the basis of this study the answer would have to be a qualified
"possibly." (9) But the amount of advertising is not closely related to
product quality. (10) Some advertised products are apparently of better
quality than some nonadvertised products, when rated by certain cri- *conch*
teria, in some years.[1]

Examine the functions of the paragraphs by looking carefully at each
sentence.
   Paragraph 1, like many opening paragraphs, raises an issue; it states
the question to be addressed. The three sentences as a group inform the
reader that the question of interest is whether advertising is a sign of higher
product quality. Frequently, first paragraphs "introduce the topic."
   In the second paragraph, sentences (4) and (5) together indicate to
the reader how product quality was measured. Thus, in this paragraph the
writer supplies an important definition.
   Paragraph 3 presents the evidence used by the writer to answer the
question raised in the first paragraph. The last paragraph restates the issue
and presents the writer's conclusion—that is, the point he wanted to make.
Sentences (8) through (10) make up the conclusion.
   We have now identified the most important organizational elements
of the passage. You should learn to highlight these in some way as you

[1]Adapted from H. J. Rotfeld and K. B. Rotzoll, "Advertising and Product Quality," *Journal
of Consumer Affairs* 10 (Summer 1976), 33–47.

read other passages. The search for the author's organization is a preliminary step in critical reading, which must occur prior to any evaluation of what you read. Some organizational elements are much more important than others. It is very important that you be aware of the process used to locate the key organizational elements. The next two chapters will teach you how to identify them.

The Structure of Expository Writing

The same organization or structure that you look for as you read should be uppermost in your mind as you write. When you compose an essay, you should be conscious of the contribution made by each sentence and by each paragraph. When teachers urge you to edit your work or rewrite first drafts, they intend that you remove sentences that do not aid your purpose.

You can examine the purpose or objective of your writing by making and then checking an outline of your intended structure. Do the sections you have planned to write all move your prospective reader toward the conclusion or thesis you intend? Will the audience you have in mind be able to comprehend your organizational pattern? After you have satisfied yourself that the target readers will grasp your basic structure, you will be ready to construct the sentences and paragraphs that will satisfy specific functions.

As you write each paragraph, think explicitly about both the roles of the sentences and the function of the paragraph as a whole. Sentences should make a contribution to the overall purpose of the paragraph in which they are located. Remove those sentences that serve no clear purpose. As you become more self-conscious about your writing, you will probably discover that much of your editing will involve removing sentences that have no evident function.

Practice Exercises

When you have completed this chapter, you should be sensitive to the need to recognize the author's organization as a preliminary step in critical reading. Moreover, at this stage of the book, we hope that you recognize that *it is essential to determine the function of each sentence and paragraph.*

In the following practice passages, try to "talk back" to the author by determining the function of each sentence; then compare your answers with ours. If you feel uncertain about the quality of your answers, don't worry. You will gain much more confidence in your thinking abilities as you read the rest of the book. Many others have learned to think carefully through this process, and so can you.

Now for some practice!

Passage 1

Background

(1) There is some speculation that schizophrenics may be biologically *why ①* different from other people. (2) Viewing this problem from the bio- ② logical perspective leads to two different kinds of questions. (3) The ? first major question is: Can it be shown that there is a hereditary factor in schizophrenia? (4) If such a factor exists, and most people agree that *y* it does, then the next step is to isolate the heredity mechanisms involved.

Thesis (5) The second major question is: What specific biological differences can be found that distinguish between people who show schizophrenic behavior and people who do not? (6) If these differences can be identified, they may lead to clues about the mechanisms that cause schizophrenic behavior.

(7) One way to understand more clearly the roles of heredity and en- *method -* vironment in producing schizophrenic behavior is to study twins. (8) There are two types of twins. (9) Identical or monozygotic (MZ) twins ✓ are produced from the same fertilized egg and are genetically identical. (10) Fraternal or dizygotic (DZ) twins are produced from two fertilized eggs and thus have the same genetic relationship as any other brothers and sisters.

(11) About a dozen major studies of twins have been carried out. (12) All show that MZ twins have a greater chance of being concordant for schizophrenia than DZ twins do. (13) (Concordance is a measure of agreement.) (14) These findings suggest an hereditary factor.

(15) However, the fact that there is less than 100 percent concordance for schizophrenia in monozygotic twins cannot be ignored. (16) It is clear that heredity alone is not enough to produce a schizophrenic disorder, at least not in most people.[2]

① conclusion
② Thesis .

Passage 2

(1) When a state-supported school adopts an unlimited-cut policy, who *statement* is the loser? (2) In essence, students who enroll in a class and have excessive absences are stealing public funds by wasting the taxpayer's *back* money and depriving other students of enrollment in the class.

(3) An analysis of my students' grade averages and absences for a 2- *meth* year period revealed that each day of absence cost the average student almost 2 points on his or her final grade. (4) Fifty-two percent of the variability in students' grades can be explained in terms of the number *concl* of absences from class.

[2]Adapted from I. G. Sarason and B. R. Sarason, *Abnormal Psychology: The Problem of Maladaptive Behavior*, 4th ed. (Englewood Cliffs, N.J.: Prentice-Hall, 1984).

(5) Rather than requiring attendance, I propose to permit students maximum freedom by requiring them to compensate the taxpayers for any unexcused absences. (6) The amount of the payment would equal that part of the educational expense not covered by student fees.[3]

Passage 3

(1) When a government decides to make it illegal to possess certain drugs, it is violating one of our basic rights—the right of privacy. (2) None of our other freedoms is valuable unless we are protected from the prying eyes and ears of the government. (3) When an American is prevented from using a drug, the majority has infringed on her right to consume in private. (4) How would the government know whether a drug was being used by Citizen Z unless it invaded her privacy? (5) It wouldn't.

(6) Even if the war on drugs were not an invasion of privacy, it would be dumb because it is an expensive fight that can never be won. (7) The government is spending an estimated $100 billion each year to stop illegal drug use. (8) Yet the same government estimates that approximately 20 percent of the population uses illegal drugs. (9) Does anyone really believe that one out of five Americans can be forced to give up the high of their choice?

———————————————— Sample Responses ————————————————

Passage 1

This passage has a structure typical of many textbook passages. The first sentence provides a brief background to the problem, while sentences (2) through (6) state two major research questions and the rationale for asking these questions. Thus, the first paragraph as a whole defines the problem or controversy. The second paragraph, sentences (7) through (10), suggests a methodology to study the problem and supplies definitions necessary to understand the methodology. Paragraph 3 summarizes results of studies and states a partial conclusion; sentences (11) and (12) describe results, sentence (13) provides a key definition, and sentence (14) states a conclusion. Sentence (15) in the final paragraph states additional evidence which provides the basis for the more complete conclusion.

[3]Adapted from D. R. Street, "Noncompulsory Attendance: Can State-Supported Universities Afford This Luxury?" *Journal of College Student Personnel* 16 (March 1975), 124–27.

Passage 2

The first sentence defines a controversy or question that motivated the writing of the remaining sentences. The second sentence then gives the author's conclusion about the controversy. Thus, the first paragraph provides the issue and the conclusion. Sentences (3) and (4) in the second paragraph provide the evidence for the conclusion. The last two sentences (paragraph 3) suggest one solution based on the assumption that the reader agrees with the conclusion in sentence (2).

Passage 3

This argument is more complex. Each paragraph presents a reason for an implied conclusion. The first paragraph argues that the government should stop regulating drug use because the regulation is a serious invasion of our privacy. The first sentence presents the argument. Sentences (2) through (5) repeat and expand on the argument in the first sentence.

The second paragraph presents the argument that since drug enforcement is so expensive and is futile, we should stop regulating drug use. Sentence (6) summarizes that argument. Sentence (7) presents evidence demonstrating how expensive drug regulation is. Sentence (8) indicates the extent of illegal use of drugs, and sentence (9) simply expresses dismay that such an extensive problem would have been regulated in the first place.

Taken together, the two paragraphs present a case against government regulation of drug use.

For the Self-Examination passages, we will not provide any sample responses. Thus, Passage 4 in each chapter gives you an opportunity to practice critical reading on your own.

Passage 4 (Self-Examination)

concl (1) For decades the defective automobile has brought us death and physical injury. (2) Before more of us are mutilated by automobile accidents, let's do something to prevent the carnage on our streets. (3) The need for action is clear. (4) Automobile accidents cost our economy over $10 billion every year in property damage, lost wages, and medical expenses.

(5) As a community we must act through our legislatures to restrict the tendency of car companies to make unsafe cars. (6) The automobile *suggestion* manufacturers will probably not make safer cars unless compelled by

law to do so. (7) A major part of their profits stems from the repair business. (8) If cars would withstand collisions with less damage, fewer repair parts would be sold. (9) Instead of recognizing their own role in the human tragedy caused by automobile accidents, executives for the automobile firms typically blame accidents on careless drivers.

III

What Are
the Issue
and the Conclusion?

Those who write editorials, books, or magazine articles are often trying to convince readers of something. What you read is often a response to some issue, question, or controversy that the writer has been thinking about, probably for a long time. To critically evaluate the writer's reasoning, you must know what that controversy is and the writer's position with respect to it. In this book we will refer to a writer's thesis or position as his *conclusion*.

When you have completed this chapter, you should be able to answer the first of our critical questions successfully.

✧ *Critical Question:* **What are the issue and the conclusion?**

Kinds of Issues

It will be helpful at this point to identify two kinds of issues you will typically encounter. The following questions illustrate one of these:

>Do obese people have emotional problems?
>Is problem-solving more effective in a large or a small group?
>Do males have dreams different from those of females?
>Can a child's IQ be raised by a stimulating environment?
>Is it true that increasing taxes tends to reduce inflation?
>Does watching violence on TV make us insensitive to crime on the streets?

All of these questions have one thing in common. They demand answers that describe the way the world is. For example, answers to the first two questions might be, "In general, obese people have emotional problems," and "Problem solving is most effective in a small group."

We will refer to arguments generated by this kind of issue as *descriptive arguments*. You will find such arguments all around you. They appear in textbooks of disciplines such as psychology, sociology, political science, economics, education, and geography; in magazines; and on television. Such arguments reflect our curiosity about patterns or order in the world.

Now let's look at examples of a second kind of question:

> Should capital punishment be abolished?
> Is it desirable to fluoridate drinking water?
> What ought to be done about unemployment?
> Should people be required to retire at a certain age?

All of these questions demand answers that suggest the way the world *ought to be*. For example, answers to the first questions might be, "Capital punishment *should be* abolished," and "We *ought to* fluoridate our drinking water."

These issues are ethical, or moral, issues; they raise questions about what is right or wrong, desirable or undesirable, good or bad. They demand prescriptive answers. Thus, we will refer to arguments generated by such issues as *prescriptive arguments*. Prescriptive arguments are typical of reasoning about social controversies, such as those surrounding abortion, marijuana, handguns, pornography, prostitution, and conservation of energy.

We have somewhat oversimplified. Sometimes it will be quite difficult to decide what kind of reasoning is being used. It will be useful to keep these distinctions in mind, however, because the kinds of critical evaluations you eventually make will differ depending upon the kind of argument to which you are responding.

What Is the Issue?

How does one go about determining the basic question or issue? Frequently it is very simple: The writer or speaker will tell you. The issue will often be identified in the body of the text, usually right at the beginning, or it may even be found in the title. If the issue is explicitly stated, you will usually find phrases such as the following:

> *The question I am raising* is whether taxes are too high in our country.
> Fluoridation of our water: *Is it the right thing to do?*
> *Should* sex education be taught in the school?
> *Why* isn't our present educational system working?
> *Does* how you sleep reveal your personality?

Unfortunately, the question is not always explicitly stated, and instead must be inferred from the conclusion. In such cases the conclusion must be found before you can identify the issue. Thus, where the question is not explicitly stated, the first step in critical evaluation is to find the conclusion—a frequently difficult step.

We cannot critically evaluate until we find the conclusion!

Let's see how we go about looking for that very important structural element.

Searching for the Author's Conclusion

To identify the conclusion, the reader must ask, What is the writer or speaker trying to prove? The answer to this question will be the conclusion.

In searching for a conclusion, you will be looking for a statement or set of statements that the author wants you to believe. The author wants you to believe the conclusion on the basis of her other statements. In short, the basic structure of persuasive writing is: *This* because of *that*. *This* refers to the conclusion; *that* refers to the support for the conclusion. This structure represents the process of *inference*. In a dispute, conclusions are *inferences*; they are derived by reasoning. Inferences are *not facts*, nor are they something we know automatically; they are beliefs which require other facts or beliefs to prove or support them.

The last paragraph says a lot. It would be a good idea for you to read it again. Understanding the nature of a conclusion is an essential step toward critical reading. Let's look closely at a conclusion and at the inference process. Here is a brief paragraph; see if you can identify the conclusion, then the statements that support it.

> We oppose a mandatory retirement age. We believe that age is an inappropriate and unreasonable basis for determining whether an individual can do a job.

The statement, "We oppose a mandatory retirement age" is this writer's answer to the question of whether there should be a mandatory retirement age; it is her conclusion. She supports the conclusion (a belief) with another belief: "We believe that age is an inappropriate and unreasonable basis for determining whether an individual can do a job." Do you see why the latter belief is not a conclusion? It is not the conclusion because it is used to prove something else. *Remember:* To believe one statement (the conclusion) because you think it is well supported by *other* beliefs is to make an inference. When people engage in this process, they are reasoning; the conclusion is the outcome of this reasoning.

Resisting the Temptation to Believe the Task Is Simple

Finding the conclusion is not as simple or obvious as it may seem at first glance. It is very common for readers to "miss the point." Writers frequently make the task difficult. For example, the writer often does not explicitly state the conclusion; it may only be implied by other statements or by the title. In other cases, many statements will have the appearance of a conclusion, but will actually serve other functions. It is important that you resist the temptation to believe that identifying the conclusion is a simple task. In the next section, we will describe ways to make certain that you have found the conclusion. *Remember:* Identifying the conclusion is crucial, and it is often not simple.

Clues to Discovery: How to Find the Conclusion

There are a number of clues to help you identify the conclusion.

CLUE No. 1: **Ask what the issue is.** Since a conclusion is always a response to an issue, it will help you to find the conclusion if you know the issue. We discussed earlier how to identify the issue. First, look at the title. Next, look at the opening paragraphs. If this technique doesn't tell you, skimming several pages may be necessary.

CLUE No. 2: **Look for indicator words.** The conclusion will frequently be preceded by *indicator words* that signify that a conclusion is coming. A list of such indicator words follows.

therefore	we may deduce that
thus	points to the conclusion that
so	the point I'm trying to make is
in short	in my opinion
it follows that	the most obvious explanation
it is believed that	it is highly probable that
shows that	in fact
indicates that	the truth of the matter is
suggests that	alas
proves that	as a result
yet	it should be clear that

When you see these indicator words, take note of them. They tell you that a conclusion may follow.

Read the following two passages and identify and highlight the indicator words. By doing so, you will have identified the statements containing the conclusion.

Passage A

But now, more than two years after voters overwhelmingly approved the lottery, it has been proven that the game is not a sure success; in fact, it can be considered a failure.

First of all, during the campaign for passage of the lottery, the public was repeatedly told that the proceeds would go toward curing the financial ills of both higher education and local primary and secondary schools. It was on this premise that the lottery received overwhelming support from the public. Not until it was approved, however, was it widely conceded that lottery profits would go into the general fund instead of the state's education budget. This means that less than half of the lottery's profits goes to education.

Passage B

When mothers smoke during pregnancy, it is highly probable that their children will read with less comprehension when they attend school. A recent study of 10,000 children born in the 1960s suggests that there is a small but statistically significant reduction in reading-comprehension scores of children whose mothers smoked when they were pregnant. The message seems to be, If you're pregnant, stop smoking!

You should have highlighted the following phrases: "it has been proven" and "in fact" in passage A, and "it is highly probable that" and "suggests that" in passage B. The conclusions follow these words.

Unfortunately, many written and spoken communications do not introduce the conclusion with indicator words. However, when *you* write, you should draw attention to your thesis with indicator words. Those words act as a neon sign drawing attention to the thesis you want the reader to accept.

CLUE No. 3: **Look in likely locations.** Conclusions tend to occupy certain locations. The first two places to look are at the beginning and at the end. Many writers begin with a statement of purpose, which contains what they are trying to prove. Others summarize their conclusions at the end. If you are reading a long, complex passage and are having difficulty seeing where it is going, skip ahead to the ending.

CLUE No. 4: **Remember what a conclusion is not.** Conclusions will not be any of the following:

Examples

Facts

Definitions

Background information

When you have identified the conclusion, check to see that is is none of these.

Dangers of Missing the Conclusion

If you miss the conclusion, you will simply be "spinning your wheels" as you try to evaluate critically. Missing the point not only leads to frustration, but frequently to unnecessary arguments, and sometimes embarrassment. All subsequent critical-questioning techniques require correct identification of the conclusion. When you have identified it, highlight it in some way. You will need to refer back to it several times as you ask further questions. As you critically evaluate, *always* keep the conclusion in mind!

Your Thesis and Effective Writing

Since readers of *your* writing will be looking for your thesis or conclusion, help them by giving it the clarity it deserves. It is the central message you want to deliver. Emphasize it; leave no doubt about what it actually is. Making your conclusion easily identifiable not only makes a reader's task easier, it also may improve the logic of your writing. By requiring yourself to define a thesis, you are more likely to provide reasoning that moves toward the single goal of a convincing conclusion. An effective way to emphasize the conclusion is to insert it at the beginning or end of your essay and precede it with an indicator word.

Practice Exercises

♢   *Critical Question:* **What are the issue and the conclusion?**

Passage 1

(1) "The United States has the world's highest standard of living. (2) It is not a utopia, but in the real world our economy is the best there is." (3) How often have you heard this statement either as an expression of national superiority or as a defense of the status quo?

(4) Alas, it is simply untrue. (5) Our country has not generated the world's highest per capita GNP since the early 1950s, when we were surpassed by Kuwait. (6) More important, perhaps, is the fact that we have been surpassed, or are about to be, by a number of countries in Europe. (7) Among industrial countries, Sweden and Switzerland can each claim to be more successful, with a per capita GNP 20 percent

above ours. (8) We have also been passed by Denmark and are about to be surpassed by Norway and West Germany. (9) Relative to achievements in the rest of the world, the United States economy no longer delivers the goods.

Passage 2

(1) Is torture, by which I mean the use of physical or mental pain to gain information, everywhere and always indefensible? (2) Certainly torturing an individual is a less grievous violation of his rights than killing him. (3) Yet in most systems of morality, killing is sometimes justified. (4) Certainly killing is more moral in the prosecution of a just war, such as World War II. (5) (Audie Murphy was held up as an example to the youth of the postwar generation for the number of Germans he killed singlehandedly, just as Sergeant Alvin York, Tennessee sharpshooter, became a folk hero following the "war to end wars.") (6) The policeman who kills in the line of duty is often seen as a hero; so is the man who takes the life of an assailant to protect his wife or children. (7) In both instances, indeed, there seems a positive moral obligation to kill a criminal rather than let an innocent human life be taken.

(8) The point I want to make is this: If there are occasions when it is morally justifiable to kill, then there are times when it is morally justifiable to inflict temporary mental or physical suffering, an infinitely less serious violation of human rights.[1]

Passage 3

(1) A long-term study of physical activity and heart disease among San Francisco-area longshoremen helps us understand the relationship between exercise and heart disease. (2) Published in the March 13, 1975 issue of the *New England Journal of Medicine*, the comprehensive report covered the experience of 6,351 men over a 22-year period. (3) Once again, vigorous activity appeared to be a significant factor. (4) Compared to workers whose jobs involved light or moderately strenuous tasks, those who engaged in the heaviest labor had a lower incidence of heart disease and only one-third the rate of sudden deaths from heart attacks. (5) The researchers concluded that vigorous exercise was a "critical factor in cardiovascular well-being especially as it would prevent sudden death from coronary heart disease."[2]

[1]Adapted from P. J. Buchanan, "The Right Time for Torture," *Skeptic* 17 (January/February 1977), 18.
[2]Adapted from "Exercise Devices," *Consumer Reports* 42 (May 1977), 255–56.

─────────────────── **SAMPLE RESPONSES** ───────────────────

Passage 1

The first paragraph introduces the issue or controversy. The second paragraph contains the writer's opinion about the issue. One indicator word is present in the second paragraph—"alas." The presence of this indicator word suggests that sentence (4) contains the conclusion. Another clue is location. Sentences (4) and (9) begin and end the paragraph where the writer provides her thesis. Both sentences give an answer to the question that identifies the issue. Thus, we have found the conclusion.

CONCLUSION: *The U.S. economy is not the best there is.*

In this passage, the issue is not explicitly stated; thus we must infer it from the author's conclusion.

ISSUE: *Which economic system is best?*

Passage 2

Sentence (1) explicitly states the issue. We know that paragraph 2 is the conclusion by the author's use of the indicator words, "The point I want to make is . . ." The conclusion follows these words. Again, note the location clues: The conclusion occurs in the last sentence, the question in the first sentence.

CONCLUSION: *If there are occasions when it is morally justifiable to kill, then there are times when it is morally justifiable to inflict temporary mental or physical suffering.*

ISSUE: *Is torture everywhere and always indefensible?*

Passage 3

An indicator word and location clues aid us in finding the conclusion in this passage. The indicator word "concluded" is found in the last sentence.

CONCLUSION: *Vigorous exercise is a critical factor in preventing death from coronary heart disease.*

ISSUE: *Does vigorous physical activity help prevent death from coronary heart disease?*

Read Identify Issue + Conclusion

Passage 4 (Self-Examination)

Everything we know about society's efforts to cope with crime suggests that we should take a very pessimistic view of people and their institutions, a view that requires a limited definition of progress.

Most serious crimes are committed by repeaters. In fact, a recent study showed that, among a large group of boys who were studied over a long period of time, chronic offenders accounted for over half of recorded delinquencies and about two-thirds of all violent crimes. While most serious crime fails to lead to an arrest, most chronic offenders eventually get arrested. Yet, many of these suffer little loss of freedom.

Given the present state of affairs, the only solution that makes sense is to imprison the chronic serious offender for a long period of time. It is obvious that such a strategy would prevent these offenders from committing additional crimes. While this strategy would not solve the crime problem, it would prevent a substantial number of serious crimes; perhaps it would lead to as much as a 20 percent reduction. Such a reduction is unlikely if society focuses upon attacking the causes of crime, since we don't have the knowledge or resources to make such an attack successful.

IV

What Are
the Reasons?

Chapter III gave you some guidelines for locating two very important parts of the structure of an argument, the issue and the conclusion. This chapter focuses on techniques for identifying the third essential element of an argument—the reasons.

When a writer has a conclusion she wants you to accept, she must present reasons to persuade you that she is right, and to show you *why*.

It is the mark of a rational person to support her beliefs by adequate proof, especially when the beliefs are of a controversial nature. For example, when someone asserts that we should abolish the CIA, this assertion should be met with the challenge, "Why do you say that?" You should raise this question whether you agree or disagree. The person's reasons may be either strong or weak, but you will not know until you have asked the question and identified the reasons. If the answer is "Because I think so," you should be dissatisfied with the argument, since the "reason" is a mere restatement of the conclusion. However, if the answer is evidence concerning wrongdoing by the CIA, you will want to consider such evidence when you evaluate the conclusion. *Remember:* You cannot determine the worth of a conclusion until you identify the reasons.

Identifying reasons is a particularly important step in critical reading and writing. An opinion cannot be evaluated fairly unless we ask why it is held and get a satisfactory response. Focusing on reasons requires us to remain open to and tolerant of views that might differ from our own. If we reacted to conclusions rather than to reasoning, we would tend to stick to the conclusions we brought to the discussion or essay, and those conclusions that agree with our own would receive our rapid assent. If we are ever to reexamine our own opinions, we must stay open to the reasons provided by those with opinions that we do not yet share.

◊   *Critical Question:*   **What are the reasons?**

Initiating the Questioning Process

The first step in identifying reasons is to approach the argument with a questioning attitude, and the first question you should ask is a *why* question. You have identified the conclusion; now you wish to know why the conclusion makes sense. If a statement does not answer the question, Why does the writer believe that?, then it is not a reason. In order to function as a reason, a statement (or group of statements) must provide support for a conclusion.

Let us apply the questioning attitude to the following paragraph. First we will find the conclusion; then we will ask the appropriate *why* question. Remember your guidelines for finding the conclusion. (The indicator words for the conclusion have been underlined.)

> (1) Is the cost of hospital care outrageous? (2) A recent survey by the American Association of Retired Persons offers reliable evidence on this issue. (3) Independent audits of the bills of 2000 patients found that hospitals overcharge their patients by an average of 15 percent. (4) In addition, exit interviews with 400 patients revealed high amounts of dismay and anger when the patients were informed about the size of their total hospital bill. (5) In short, the costs of hospital care are higher than the services provided warrant. *conclusion*

What follows "In short" answers the question raised in statement (1). Thus, the conclusion is statement (5), ". . . the costs of hospital care are higher than the services provided warrant." *Highlight the conclusion!*

We then ask the question, Why does the author believe the conclusion? The statements that answer that question are the reasons. In this particular case, the author provides us with evidence as reasons. Statements (3) and (4) jointly provide the evidence; that is, together they provide support for the conclusion. Together they serve as the reason for the conclusion.

Now, try to find the reasons in the following paragraph. Again, first find the conclusion, highlight it, and then ask the *why* question.

> (1) Euthanasia is detrimental to the welfare of society because it destroys man's ideas of sacrifice, loyalty, and courage in bearing pain. (2) Some dying persons accept their suffering as a way of paying for their sins. (3) These people should be permitted to die as they wish—without help from any other person in speeding up the dying process.

There is no obvious indicator word for the conclusion in the paragraph, but the author is clearly arguing against the morality of euthanasia. The conclusion here is: "Euthanasia is detrimental to the welfare of society." Why does the author believe this? Her major reason is that "it destroys man's ideas of sacrifice, loyalty, and courage in bearing pain." The next two sentences in the excerpt provide additional support for this reason.

One of the best ways for you to determine whether you have discovered a writer's reasons is to try to play the role of the writer. Put yourself in the position of the writer, and ask yourself, Why am I in favor of this conclusion that I am supporting? Try to put into your own words how you believe the writer would answer this question. If you can do this, you have probably discovered the writer's reasons.

Identifiers

Words That Identify Reasons

As was the case with conclusions, there are certain words that will typically indicate that a reason will follow. *Remember:* The structure of an argument is, *This, because of that.* Thus, the word *because*, as well as words synonymous with and similar in function to it, will frequently signal the presence of reasons. A list of indicator words for reasons follows.

because	in view of the fact that
first—second	for the reason that
since	is supported by
for	for example
for one thing	also

Find the reasons in the following passage by identifying the indicator words.

(1) No one could be more willing to recommend hunting as a wholesome form of outdoor recreation than I. (2) For one thing, I believe that hunting has great value for those who participate in it. (3) It is a form of recreation that brings many physical, mental, and even spiritual benefits to the individual. (4) Hunting also develops self-reliance and confidence.

You should have identified statements (2) and (3) jointly as one reason, and (4) as another. Did you notice the indictor words "for one thing" and "also"?

Kinds of Reasons

There are several different kinds of reasons, depending on the kind of issue. Many reasons will be statements presenting *evidence*. By evidence we mean facts, data, or statistics. When a speaker or writer is trying to support a descriptive conclusion, the answer to the *why* question will typically be evidence. The following example provides a descriptive argument; find the author's reasons.

> (1) The fact is that despite radical changes in the educational and occupational opportunities available to women, they remain as underrepresented as do members of many minority groups in high-status professional or executive positions. (2) Although women constitute 40 percent of the labor force and control, at least in name, 82 percent of the country's wealth, their participation in business and industry is perhaps summarized by the titles of two articles in a recent issue of *Business World*: "The Men at the Top: Business World Speaks with Thirty Industry Leaders," and "The Women at the Top: Business World Speaks with Two Senior Vice Presidents at Macy's."[1]

You should have identified the first statement as the conclusion. It is a descriptive statement about the number of women in professional or executive positions. The rest of the paragraph presents the evidence—the reason for the conclusion. *Remember:* The conclusion itself will not be evidence; it will be a belief supported by evidence or by other beliefs.

In prescriptive arguments, reasons are typically either prescriptive or descriptive statements. The use of these two kinds of statements to support a conclusion in a prescriptive argument is illustrated in the following:

> (1) With regard to the big controversy over grade inflation, I would like to ask a few questions. (2) What difference does it make if the people who are really good are never distinguished from the average student? (3) Is there a caste system in our society according to grade-point averages?

> (4) Are those with high point averages superior to those with low point averages? (5) In the majority of cases, grades are not a true indication of learning, anyway; they are a measure of how well a student can absorb information for a short time period and regurgitate it on a test.

---

[1] C. Millsom, "Women and Education," *Educational Leadership* (November 1973), 99–101.

(6) Students will retain the information that interests them and is important anyway. (7) Why can't we eliminate grades and be motivated only by the inborn curiosity and zest for learning that is really in us all?

The controversy here is what to do about grade inflation. The author's solution to the problem is to abolish grades, as indicated in sentence (7). Let's look for sentences that answer the question, Why does she believe this conclusion? First, note that no evidence is presented. Sentences (2) and (3) jointly form one reason: It is not important to distinguish the average student from the good student. Note that this is a prescriptive statement; it indicates the writer's view about how the world should be. Sentences (4) and (5) add a second reason: Grades are not a true indicator of learning. This is a descriptive statement regarding a disadvantage of grades. Sentence (6) provides a third reason: Students will retain only the information that interests them and is important anyway (grades do not help learners to remember). This is another descriptive statement.

Keeping the Reasons and Conclusions Straight

As you read critically, the reasons and the conclusion are the most important elements to bring into clear focus. Many arguments are long and not very well organized. Sometimes a set of reasons will support one conclusion, and that conclusion will function as the main reason for another conclusion. Reasons may be supported by other reasons. In especially complicated arguments, it is frequently difficult to keep the structure straight in your mind as you attempt to critically evaluate what you have read. To overcome this problem, try to develop your own organizing procedure for keeping the reasons and conclusions separate and in a logical pattern.

Some readers have found the following suggestions useful:

1. Underline the reasons and conclusion in different colors of ink, or highlight the conclusion and underline the reasons.
2. Label the reasons and conclusion in the margin.
3. For long passages, make a list of reasons at the end of the essay.
4. For especially complicated reasoning, diagram the structure, using numbers to refer to each reason and conclusion, and arrows to designate the direction of relationship. Sometimes this technique is most effective if all reasons and conclusions are first paraphrased in the margins, then numbered.

We can illustrate these suggested techniques by attempting to find the conclusion and reasons in the following relatively complex passage.

(1) Do physicians have a moral obligation to provide free medical care for those who cannot pay? (2) *Yes, they do.* (3) <u>First</u>, society has restricted most medical practice to physicians. (4) <u>Since</u> the resultant medical monopoly has obvious economic benefits, (5) <u>it seems reasonable that</u> the profession acknowledge its collective responsibility to provide care even to those who cannot pay.

(6) <u>Second</u>, the moral obligation of individual physicians to provide free care derives from an understanding of their special role. (7) Physicians should not be compared to plumbers or car mechanics, or to other craftsmen who repair inanimate objects. (8) Unlike automobile repairs, the health problems of people are not deferrable or negotiable. (9) That doctors help some people without pay is essential if doctors are to remain doctors and medical services are not to be regarded as just another form of profit-seeking business activity.[2]

Initially you should notice that we have underlined the conclusion and key indicator words. As you read this passage, you surely noticed that the reasoning structure is quite complicated. For such a passage, we have to understand the logical sequence of sentences to isolate the reasoning structure. Thus we have diagrammed the relationships among the reasons and conclusion. Try to diagram this passage on your own; then, compare your diagram to ours.

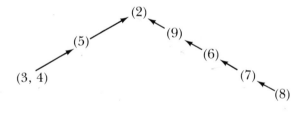

Our diagram reflects our interpretation that sentence (5) in paragraph 2 and sentence (9) in paragraph 3 directly answered the question, Why is the conclusion, sentence (2), true? The direction of the rest of the arrows in the diagram denotes how we believe these two reasons are supported by further reasons. For example, statements (3) and (4) jointly provide support for (5).

Diagramming is useful for gaining an understanding of especially complicated arguments. When reading lengthy essays it is always useful to paraphrase the main reasons in the margins. Thus, for the above passage, we might have supplied the following paraphrased reasons:

[2]Adapted from M. Siegler, "Treating the Jobless for Free: Do Doctors Have a Special Duty? Yes," *The Hastings Center Report* (August 1983), 12–13.

Paragraph 1: Physicians owe a debt to society.

Paragraph 2: The physician's role is special; physicians are unlike businessmen.

We have mentioned a number of techniques for you to use in developing a clear picture of the reasoning structure. If some other technique works better for you, by all means use it. The important point is to keep the reasons and conclusion straight as you prepare to evaluate.

Reasons and Effective Writing

When you are writing, you will usually want to make your reader's job as easy as possible. Thus, your task is to use words, sentences, paragraphs, and indicator words to illuminate the logical relationships in your argument.

A good way to begin is by clearly outlining or diagramming your reasoning structure. Then keep several fundamental rules in mind as you write. The first is the rule of *grouping*: Keep reasons for the same conclusion together. You can do this by keeping grammatical structure parallel and by using appropriate indicator words. The second is the rule of *direction*. After you have developed a sequential order of reasons, such that each reason relates to a subsequent one, word your essay so that the reasons move in a single direction. For example, a sequence that follows the rule of direction goes from the final conclusion to its main reason to the reason for that reason.

A third rule is that of keeping reasons that bear a similar relationship to the conclusion in close proximity to one another, so that their relationship is easy to see. Do not separate them with reasons that involve quite different considerations.

Practice Exercises

◊   *Critical Question:*   **What are the reasons?**

First survey the passage and highlight its conclusion. Then ask the question, Why?, and locate the reasons. Use indicator words to help. Keep the conclusions and the reasons separate.

Passage 1

A 3-year-old picked up a .356 magnum the other day and killed a 7-year-old friend. According to one child who saw the murder, "He just stood there with a big hole in his stomach and blood all over the place. Then he fell over."

Just a few days later, a Chicago toy designer strolled into work carrying a handgun. He shot five people, killed three of them, and then killed himself.

Between 1966 and 1972, 44,000 Americans were killed in Vietnam. In the same period, 52,000 Americans were killed by handguns in the United States.

A recent Harris poll found that 77 percent of the American people favor federal registration of all handguns. Registration—not the namby-pamby gun controls we have now, which do so little good.

You'd think that when 77 percent of the people favor something, Congress would pass it. It hasn't, of course, despite years of overwhelming public support for such measures. It is cowed by an organized minority—the gun manufacturers and their ally, the American Rifle Association. It is a classic case of the small minority using organized political pressure for selfish ends.

And it is killing us. One by one, day by day. Just read your newspaper.

Passage 2

Eunice Kennedy Shriver stood up for parents on the Op-Ed page of the *Washington Post* recently. In a piece entitled, "Yes, Parents Should Know," she supported the Health and Human Services Department's proposed rule to require that federally funded family-planning clinics notify the parents of minors to whom they are providing prescription contraceptives.

Mrs. Shriver's arguments for the proposed rule, which echo the administration's, reveal much well-meaning intent and a distorted view of reality. Mandatory notification is more likely to deter girls from using the clinic than to benefit girls who come home to find their parents reading a government notice announcing that their daughter has obtained birth control.

The premise behind mandatory notification is that adolescent knowledge of human sexuality causes adolescent promiscuity. No evidence has yet been offered that can support this premise. Indeed, the June report by the Alan Guttmaker Institute found that sex education in schools does not promote promiscuity in teenagers, and may even discourage teenage pregnancy. Planned Parenthood does not introduce teenagers to sex; girls who come to this clinic have been having sex for an average of nine months before their first visit.[3]

[3]Adapted from A. Shlaes, "The Squeal Squawk," *The New Republic* (August 9, 1982), 18–20.

Passage 3

Even though concern about the improvement of instruction occupies a great amount of the time and energy of many faculty and administrators, and articles about faculty development that focus on improving teaching and learning fill the current publications in American higher education, there is still reason to believe that very few people genuinely care. The real question, as always, is: Does improved teaching really count?

In a survey entitled *Assessing Faculty Performance* (Teaching Research Division, Oregon State System of Higher Education, November 1976), conducted among all faculty in the Oregon system of higher education, college faculty listed as the most important factors for promotion: advanced degrees, department chairman evaluations, time in academic rank, and personality traits.

In a similar study at the University of Nebraska in 1975–76, Patricia Cross discovered that of the nine possible criteria for promotion, the number of publications was considered the most important, and only 28 percent of the faculty were willing to have colleagues visit their classes.

When the judgments are made, teaching does not seem to be among the critical criteria considered in determining faculty advancement.[4]

———————————— SAMPLE RESPONSES ————————————

Passage 1

ISSUE: *Do we need federal handgun control legislation?*

CONCLUSION: *We need federal handgun control legislation.*

REASONS: 1. *Handguns are responsible for many deaths.*
2. *Handgun availability makes killing easier.*
3. *The majority of the American people favored federal legislation.*
4. *Pressure from a small minority has kept the law from being passed.*

Note: We have identified the reasons we think the author would have listed if we had asked him the question, "Why do you believe we need federal handgun legislation?" We may not think he *should* have included certain reasons, but at this stage of analysis, it is useful to list anything that

[4]L. R. Meeth, "Does Anybody Care?" *Change* 9 (July 1977), 4–5.

the writer may have been using as a reason. Later we will judge their appropriateness.

Passage 2

ISSUE: *Should federally funded family-planning clinics be required to notify the parents of minors to whom they are providing prescription contraceptives?*

CONCLUSION: *No, they should not be required to do so.*

REASONS: 1. *The rule is likely to deter girls from using the clinic.*
2. *There is no evidence that knowledge of human sexuality causes adolescent promiscuity.*

Passage 3

ISSUE: *Is improved teaching rewarded in universities and colleges?*

CONCLUSION: *No, improved teaching does not count.*

REASONS: 1. *A survey shows college and university faculty do not list teaching as an important factor for promotion.*
2. *A second survey shows that the number of faculty publications is considered the most important criterion for promotion and that few faculty are willing to permit colleagues to visit their classes.*

Passage 4 (Self-Examination)

The case for transplanting organs such as the heart and liver is obvious. Yet I don't buy it. For one thing, the cultural and religious significance of certain organs differs greatly among people. Because of this difference, great psychological harm might result from transplanting one person's heart into the body of another person who will always be wondering about the worth of the donor. In the case of an ovary transplant, there is another factor weakening the case for transplants. Any woman willing to subject herself to such high medical risks must have an abnormal psychological drive to produce children with her own body. Should society contribute to these psychological problems by encouraging organ transplants?

V

What Words
or Phrases
Are Ambiguous?

The first four chapters of this book have been devoted to helping you identify the basic structural elements in any essay. At this point, if you can locate a writer's conclusion and reasons, you are progressing rapidly toward the ultimate goal of forming your own rational decisions. Your next step is to put this structural picture into clearer focus.

While identifying the conclusion and reasons gives you the basic visible structure, you still need to examine the precise *meaning* of these parts before you can react fairly to the ideas being presented. You need now to pay much more attention to the details of the language. Specific words and phrases may have several different meanings or implications—that is, they may be *ambiguous*. How they are interpreted will often affect how acceptable the reasoning is to you. Consequently, before you can determine the extent to which you wish to accept one conclusion or another, you must first attempt to discover the precise meaning of the conclusion and the reasons. While their meaning typically *appears* obvious, it often is not.

The discovery and clarification of meaning require conscious, step-by-step procedures. This chapter suggests one set of such procedures. It focuses on the following question:

◊   *Critical Question:*   **What words or phrases are ambiguous?**

The Confusing Flexibility of Words

Our language is highly complex. If each word had only one potential meaning about which we all agreed, effective communication would be more likely. However, most words have more than one meaning.

Consider the multiple meanings of such words as *freedom*, *obscenity*, and *happiness*. These multiple meanings can create serious problems in determining the worth of an argument. For example, when someone argues that a magazine should not be published because it is obscene, you cannot evaluate the argument until you know what the writer means by "obscene." In this brief argument, it is easy to find the conclusion and the supporting reason, but the quality of the reasoning is difficult to judge because of the ambiguous use of *obscene*. Thus, even when you can identify the structure of what others are saying, you still must struggle with the meaning of certain words in that structure. A warning: *We often misunderstand what we read because we presume that what words mean is obvious.* Whenever you are reading, force yourself to search for ambiguity; otherwise, you may simply miss the point.

As an illustration of potential problems caused by ambiguity, take a look at the following argument; then write out the "obvious" meaning of the term *social worth*.

> More and more of us are being kept alive for extended periods of time by medical wizardry. This development is causing a strain on pension plans and social security. Unfortunately, our economy seems unable to meet both the expensive needs of the aged and the resource claims made by every other group in society. Hence, I wish to propose that we change our attitude toward the ultimate desirability of a long life. Instead, we should think in terms of the quality of life. At any point in a person's life at which his or her social worth has become minimal, we should relax our fear of suicide. Those adults who choose to escape the potential misery of old age should be permitted to do so without the rebuke of those who survive them.

How did you do? What the author is suggesting isn't clear at all, because we don't know whether he thinks that *social worth* means 1) the economic contribution that a person can make, *or* 2) the benefits of human communication and interaction. Does it really matter which of these possible interpretations you use? It certainly does. The argument would be more persuasive if the writer meant the second definition. If he intended the first definition, then he is advocating a major social change based on a very narrow concept of what it means to be human. Notice that the clues about the meaning of the term are sketchy at best. Until we find out that meaning, we aren't well prepared to form a reaction to the argument.

Such ambiguity forces the reader to make a choice from among potential meanings. This choice is required because words are so flexible, and we frequently fail to make it clear what we truly mean by a word or group of words with multiple meanings. The decision about the precise meaning of key words or phrases is an essential prerequisite to deciding whether to agree with someone's opinion. If you fail to check for ambiguity, you may react to an opinion the author never intended.

Locating Ambiguity

Can you locate the ambiguity in the following advertisement?

High-Pruf Gin: A Gift He Will Remember

How will he remember this gift? Notice that the advertisement could mean that the recipient of the gin will recall the great taste, or that he will remember the hangover the gift provided, or that he will reflect on the thought that went into choosing such a terrific gift.

Unfortunately, important instances of ambiguity are usually much more difficult to identify, and the most likely interpretation is not obvious. A major obstacle to locating ambiguity is assuming that the writer and you mean the same thing. Thus, start your search for ambiguity by trying to avoid "mind-reading."

When searching for ambiguity, you should keep in mind *why* you are looking. Someone wants you to accept a conclusion. Therefore, you are looking only for ambiguity that will affect whether or not you accept the conclusion. So, look for ambiguity in the *reasons* and in the *conclusion*!

Another useful guide in looking for ambiguity is to keep in mind the following rule: The more *abstract* a word or phrase, the more likely it is to be ambiguous. To avoid being ambiguous in our use of the term *abstract*, we define it here in the following way: A term becomes more and more abstract as it refers less and less to particular, specific instances. Thus, the words *equality*, *responsibility*, *pornography*, and *aggression* are much more abstract than are the phrases "having equal access to necessities of life," "directly causing an event," "pictures of male and female genitals," and "doing deliberate physical harm to another person." These phrases provide a much more concrete picture and therefore are less ambiguous.

When you first start trying to find ambiguity, begin by asking yourself what each word in the conclusion and reasons means, with special emphasis on the most abstract words. Could any of the words have a different meaning?

You can be certain that you have identified an important ambiguity by performing the following test. If you can express two or more alternative meanings for a term, each of which makes sense in the context of the argument, *and* if these alternative meanings would lead to different conclusions depending on which meaning is assumed, then you have located a significant ambiguity.

For instance, look at the following advertisement:

Lucky Smokes put it all together and got taste with only 3 mg. tar.

The word *taste* is ambiguous. How do we know? Let's perform the test together. Taste could mean many things. It could mean a barely noticeable mild tobacco flavor. It could mean a rather harsh, bitter flavor. Or it could have many other meanings. Isn't it true that you would be more eager to follow the advice of the advertisement if the taste provided matched your taste preference? Thus, the ambiguity is significant since it affects the degree to which you might be persuaded by the ad.

Advertising is often full of ambiguity. Advertisers intentionally engage in ambiguity in order to persuade you that their products are superior to those of their competitors. They want you to choose the meaning of ambiguous terms that is personally most desirable. Here are some sample advertising claims that are ambiguous. See if you can identify alternative, plausible meanings for the italicized words or phrases.

> **No-Pain is the *extra-strength* pain reliever.**
> **Parvu: Sensual . . . but not *too far from innocence*.**
> **Ray Rhinestone's new album: an album of *experiences*.**
> **Vital Hair Vitamins show you *what* vitamins can do for your hair.**
> **Here is a book at last that shows you how to find and keep a *good man*.**

In each case, the advertiser hoped that you would assign the most attractive meaning to the ambiguous words. Critical reading can sometimes protect you from making purchasing decisions that you would later regret.

Let's now look at a more complicated example of ambiguity. Remember that the first step is to highlight the conclusion and reasons.

> It is time to take active steps in reducing the amount of violence on television. The adverse effect of such violence is clear, as evidenced by many recent research studies. Several studies indicate that heavy TV watchers tend to overestimate the danger of physical violence in real life. Other studies show that children who are heavy TV watchers can become desensitized to violence in the real world. Numerous other studies demonstrate the adverse effect of TV violence.

This essay argues that we ought to take steps to reduce the amount of TV violence because such violence has an adverse effect. The writer then uses research evidence to support this reasoning. Let's examine the paragraph for any words or phrases that would affect our willingness to accept her reasoning.

First, notice that her conclusion is itself ambiguous. Exactly what does it mean to "take active steps in reducing the amount of violence." Does it mean to impose a legal ban against showing any act of physical violence, or might it mean putting public pressure on the networks to restrict violent episodes to late evening hours? Before you could decide whether to agree with the writer, you would first have to decide what it is she wants us to believe.

Next, look closely at her reasoning. She argues that heavy TV watchers "overestimate the danger of physical violence in real life" and "become desensitized to violence in the real world." But how much TV does one have to watch to qualify as a heavy TV watcher? Also, what does it mean to overestimate the danger of physical violence, or to become desensitized? Try to create a mental picture of what these phrases represent. If you can't, the phrases are ambiguous. You can see that if you accept this writer's argument without requiring her to clarify these ambiguous phrases, you will not have understood what it is you agreed to believe.

Context and Ambiguity

Writers and speakers only rarely define their terms. Thus, typically your only guide to the meaning of an ambiguous statement is the *context* in which the words are used. By *context*, we mean the writer's background in addition to the words and statements preceding and following the possible ambiguity. These two elements provide clues to the meaning of a potential ambiguity.

If you were to see the term *human rights* in an essay, you should immediately ask yourself, What rights are those? If you examine the context and find that the writer is a leading member of the Soviet government, it is a good bet that the human rights he has in mind are the rights to be employed, receive free health care, and obtain adequate housing. An American senator might mean something very different by human rights. She could have in mind freedoms of speech, religion, travel, and peaceful assembly. Notice that the two versions of human rights are not necessarily consistent. A country can guarantee one form of human rights, and at the same time violate the other. You must try to clarify the ambiguity surrounding the topic by examining the context in which the opinion is given.

Writers frequently make clear their assumed meaning of a term by their arguments. The following paragraph is an example.

> Studies show that most people who undergo psychotherapy benefit from the experience. In fact, a recent study shows that after ten sessions of psychotherapy, two-thirds of participants reported experiencing less anxiety.

The phrase "benefit from the experience" is potentially ambiguous, because it could have a variety of meanings. However, the writer's argument makes clear that *in this context*, "benefit from the experience" means reporting less anxiety.

Ambiguity, Definitions, and the Dictionary

It should be obvious from the preceding discussion that, to locate and clarify ambiguity, you must be aware of the possible meanings of words. Meanings usually come in one of three forms: synonyms, examples, and what we will call "definition by specific criteria." For example, one could offer at least three different definitions of *anxiety*.

1. Anxiety is feeling nervous. (*synonym*)
2. Anxiety is what Walter Mondale experienced when he turned on the television to watch the election returns. (*example*)
3. Anxiety is a subjective feeling of discomfort accompanied by increased sensitivity of the autonomic nervous system. (*specific criteria*)

For critical evaluation of most controversial issues, synonyms and examples are inadequate. They fail to tell you the specific properties that are crucial for an unambiguous understanding of the term. The most useful definitions are those that specify criteria for usage—and the more specific the better.

Where do you go for your definitions? One obvious and very important source is your dictionary. However, dictionary definitions frequently consist of synonyms, examples, or incomplete specifications of criteria for usage. These definitions often do not adequately define the use of a term in a particular essay. In such cases, you must discover possible meanings from the context of the passage, or from what else you know about the topic. We suggest you keep a dictionary handy, but keep in mind that the appropriate definition may not be there.

Let's take a closer look at some of the inadequacies of a dictionary definition. Examine the following brief sentence.

> Education is not declining in quality at this university. In my interviews,
> I found that an overwhelming majority of the students and instructors
> responded that they saw no decline in the quality of education here.

It is clearly important to know what is meant by "quality of education" in the above paragraph. If you look up the word *quality* in the dictionary, you will find many meanings, the most appropriate, given this context, being *excellence* or *superiority*. *Excellence* and *superiority* are synonyms for *quality*—and they are equally abstract. You still need to know precisely what is meant by *excellence* or *superiority*. How do you know whether education is high in quality or excellence? Ideally, you would want the writer to tell you precisely what *behaviors* he is referring to when he uses the phrase "quality of education." Can you think of some different ways that the phrase might be defined? The following list presents some possible definitions of *quality of education*:

> Average grade-point average of students
> Ability of students to think critically
> Number of professors who have doctoral degrees
> Amount of work usually required to pass an exam

Each of these definitions suggests a different way to measure quality; each specifies a different criterion. Each provides a precise way in which the term could be used. Note also that each of these definitions will affect the degree to which the reason supports the conclusion. For example, if you believe that "quality" in the conclusion refers to the ability of students to think critically, and most of the students in the interviews are defining it as how much work is required to pass an exam, the reason would not necessarily support the conclusion. Exams may not require the ability to think critically.

Thus, in many arguments you will not be able to find adequate dictionary definitions, and the context may not make the meaning clear. One way to discover possible alternative meanings is to try to create a mental picture of what the words represent. If you cannot do so, then you probably have identified an important ambiguity. Let's apply such a test to the following example.

> Welfare programs have not succeeded. They have not provided the poor with productive jobs.

The provision of productive jobs for the poor is the standard being used here to assess the worth of welfare programs. Can you create a single clear mental picture of *productive jobs*? Are there alternative definitions? Does *productive* mean "leading to greater profit" or "providing a sense of self-worth"? If you wanted to check on the accuracy of the reasoning, wouldn't you first need to know when a job is productive? You cannot count those jobs that are productive until the meaning of productive jobs is clarified. Thus, we have located an important ambiguity.

Limits of Your Responsibility to Clarify Ambiguity

After you have attempted to identify and clarify ambiguity, what can you do if you are still uncertain about the meaning of certain key ideas? What is a reasonable next step? We suggest you ignore any reason that contains ambiguity that makes it impossible to judge the acceptability of the reason. It is your responsibility as an active learner to ask questions that clarify ambiguity. However, your responsibility stops at that point. It is the writer who is trying to convince you of something. Her role as a persuader requires her to respond to your concerns about possible ambiguity.

You are not required to react to ideas or opinions that are unclear. If a friend tells you that you should enroll in a class because it "really is different," but cannot tell you how it is different, then you have no basis for agreeing or disagreeing with the advice. No one has the right to be believed if he cannot provide you with a clear picture of his reasoning.

Ambiguity and Equivocation

Equivocation is a special form of ambiguity that critical thinkers watch for. Equivocation occurs when the same words or phrases are used more than once in an argument; their meaning is changed, but you are not told that this shift has occurred. The following argument presents an example.

> *Joe:* Most of the people in this country have security. Very few Americans are having serious difficulties obtaining food, clothing, and shelter.

> *Max:* It is not true that most Americans are secure. Our industrialized, technological society creates so much dependence upon others that it is impossible to feel that we have personal control over our welfare.

While a number of potentially ambiguous words are used in this interchange (namely, "serious difficulties," "security," and "welfare"), one word is being used equivocally—"security." Joe has one meaning in mind—availability of material goods. Max has another—a sense of personal control over our well-being. The meaning of the word has shifted. Joe and Max are essentially responding to different issues. If you accept Joe's definition, Max's argument becomes irrelevant to the issue. Max's conclusion does not follow, given Joe's definition.

How does one spot an equivocation error? Look for repeated reference to the same term, and see if the term is being used consistently. When you spot an equivocation error, you have found a reason that will not be relevant to the conclusion.

Ambiguity and Effective Writing

Although most of this chapter is addressed to you as a critical reader, it is also extremely relevant to improved writing. Effective writers strive for clarity. They review their writing several times, looking for any statements that might be ambiguous.

Look back at the section on "Locating Ambiguity." Use the hints given there for finding important ambiguity to revise your own writing. For instance, abstractions that are ambiguous can be clarified by concrete illustrations that convey the meaning you intend. Pay special attention to the reason and conclusion in any essay you write; ambiguity can be an especially serious problem in those elements.

Thinking about the characteristics of your intended audience can help you decide where ambiguities need to be clarified. Jargon or specific abstractions that would be very ambiguous to a general audience may be adequately understood by a specialized audience. Remember that the reader will probably not struggle for a long time with your meaning. If you confuse your reader, you will probably lose her quickly. If you never regain her attention, then you have failed in your task as a writer.

Practice Exercises

◊   *Critical Question:*   **What words or phrases are ambiguous?**

In the following practice passages, identify instances of ambiguity. As a check on yourself, attempt to show (a) how the words that you have claimed are ambiguous have multiple meanings, and (b) how different interpretations of the words lead to different conclusions.

Passage 1

Comparable worth is the civil rights issue of the future, according to the Department of Labor. Women workers are generally unhappy about the size of their salaries compared to those of men. Such dissatisfaction is understandable, since the average wage of a female worker is only 66 percent of that of the average male worker.

However, differences in wages do not automatically imply that female workers' worth is being undervalued. Envy is not an adequate reason to ask courts and legislatures to require that women workers be paid more than they are actually worth. Our society has spoken on the relative worth of workers. Women should accept the consensus view of their worth and try to increase that worth in the future. Only then might their work be of comparable value to that of men.

Passage 2

I approve of sexual experimentation for the following reasons:

a. It is infinitely less dangerous than such sports as horseback riding, skiing, surfboarding, and automobiling. And in many respects cheaper.

b. Sexual experimentation helps to strengthen one's character, in that such activity gives the experimenter wonderful practice in not giving a damn about what certain nosey puritans think about you.

c. It provides learning and practice through which an unmarried person may become sexually experienced and competent.

d. Sexual experimentation is one of the best pathways left today for adventure, experimenting, and interpersonal experiencing.[1]

Passage 3

We should treat drug taking in the same way we treat speech and religion, as a fundamental right. No one has to ingest any drug he does not want, just as no one has to read a particular book. Insofar as the state assumes control over such matters, it can only be in order to subjugate its citizens—by protecting them from temptations as befits children, and by preventing them from exercising self-determination over their lives as befits slaves.[2]

SAMPLE RESPONSES

Passage 1

CONCLUSION: *Comparable-worth laws should be rejected.*

REASONS: *1. Envy is not an appropriate justification for such laws.*
2. The relative worth of female and male workers has already been agreed on.

This argument is unclear because the author does not define the concept of worth. Any decision about the merit of comparable-worth reforms requires a careful definition of worth. For instance, does worth refer to the monetary value of one's output, the number of people one supervises, the training required for one's job, the contribution one makes to achieving national goals, or to some combination of these? All these definitions are

---

[1]Adapted from A. Ellis, in *Sexual Latitude: For and Against*, ed. H. Hart (New York: Hart, 1971), pp. 67–70.
[2]Adapted from T. Szasz, "A Different Dose for Different Folks," *Skeptic* (January/February 1977), 47.

reasonable. But our reaction to the author's defense of current wage differences must await our understanding what he means by the worth such differences claim to measure.

Passage 2

CONCLUSION: *Sexual experimentation is desirable.*

REASONS: *1. It is cheaper and less dangerous than many other widely accepted physical activities.*
2. It is character building.
3. It enables one to learn how to have better sexual experiences.
4. It is adventurous and exciting.

The concept of sexual experimentation is not clearly specified. This ambiguity is significant because the worth of the argument is dependent on a particular meaning of *sexual experimentation*. To many people, sexual experimentation may not refer to sexual intercourse; however, the author's arguments appear to be based on a definition of sexual experimentation as sexual intercourse. For a reader who is trying to determine the worth of the conclusion, it would have been helpful if Ellis had specified more clearly which version of sexual experimentation he has in mind. For example, the psychological danger of premarital sex may be quite different depending on what type of sexual experimentation is being discussed.

The word *dangerous* in the first reason is another relevant ambiguity; one could argue, for example, that risking pregnancy is quite dangerous.

Passage 3

CONCLUSION: *Drugs should be available for those who desire them.*

REASON: *Using drugs is a voluntary choice, and to regulate drug consumption is to treat citizens as children by not permitting them to make the choice.*

Is it clear what is meant by drug taking? If drug taking refers to the ingestion of drugs that are not considered highly addictive, such as marijuana, wouldn't you be more likely to accept the reasoning than if the author included heroin within his definition of drugs? Can you tell from the argument whether the author is referring to all drugs or only to a subset of currently regulated drugs? To be able to agree or disagree with the author requires in this instance a more careful definition of what is meant by *drugs*.

Passage 4 (Self-Examination): Complex Passage

Power and Psychiatry[3]

THOMAS S. SZASZ

Psychiatry is seen frequently as concerned only with illness and its treatment, unrelated to power. Such is not the case. Informally, power might be defined as the ability of a person, group, or institution to make someone do something he does not want to do. The formal, political definition of power is, however, more important for our present purposes. Formally, power is the ability to invoke the force of the state to make someone do something or to make him stop doing something. The best example of that sort of power is the criminal law.

Actually, there are two basic ways in which a person can be deprived of liberty in the United States. One is by breaking the criminal law; if someone does that, he may get locked up in prison. The other is by breaking the mental hygiene law; if someone does that, he may get locked up in a mental hospital. Some would say that people get locked up in mental hospitals because they are sick and need treatment. Words are important, and most words prejudge the subject to which they are applied. If one calls psychiatric confinement "hospitalization," that implies it is good; if one calls it "imprisonment," that implies it is bad. Therefore, let us call it "loss of liberty." A person committed to a mental hospital cannot leave the building. In the United States today more people are locked up in mental hospitals than in prisons, despite the fact that the number of mental hospital inmates has decreased dramatically during the past decade to two.

Why is that? What are the justifications, in a free society such as ours, for depriving of liberty people who have not broken the law? To be sure, some people who end up in mental hospitals have broken the law; instead of charging them with a crime, the authorities commit them as crazy. These are not the people with whom I am concerned here.

Typically, the person who is committed to a mental hospital has not broken the law. He is locked up because he has what is called a "major mental illness"—such as depression or schizophrenia—and because he is said to be "dangerous to himself or others." I believe there is no such thing as mental illness. Mental illness is just a convenient name to pin on someone, especially if one wants to put him away in the madhouse. Take depression. Whatever depression is, it is obvious that it is not

[3]From "Power and Psychiatry," by Thomas Szasz. Published by permission of Transaction, Inc. from SOCIETY, Vol. 18, No. 4, Copyright © 1981 by Transaction, Inc.

illegal and not an illness. That feelings of sadness or futility are neither pleasant nor good does not make them sick or criminal. Not everything that is painful or unpleasant in life is an illness or a crime. It is precisely because of this simple fact that words like *depression* and *schizophrenia* are so important: they give unsuspecting people the impression, which is totally false, that certain persons exhibiting certain unpleasant behaviors are sick. The belief that such persons are crazy and do not know what is in their own best interests makes it seem legitimate to incarcerate them. This is a socially useful arrangement: it allows some people to dispose of some other people who annoy or upset them.

Obviously, any such arrangement would, in its actual implementation, affect some individuals or groups more than others. Who are the people most affected? The powerless. That is why poor people, uneducated people, people who do not speak the language well, children, and the very old are the people most likely to be committed. This was always the case, and it still is. The poor, the old, and the young are committed to mental hospitals—not because they have more schizophrenia and depression than others, nor because they are more dangerous than others, but because they have less power than others. How often are psychiatrists or lawyers committed? I suppose it happens, but I have never heard of such a case.

Commitment is a form of social control. And, in principle, social controls are not necessarily bad. There can be no society without them. Whether a particular form of social control is good or bad depends on what sort of society we want or like. It is meaningless to assert that a particular kind of social control is bad unless we have a clear idea about what sort of moral and political order, of rights and duties, we consider to be good. I think that psychiatric social controls—epitomized by commitment—are bad.

One of the fundamental moral choices people must make is between freedom and order, between individual liberty and social tranquility. As a rule, we cannot have social arrangements that maximize both. If we have more of one, we may have to be satisfied with less of the other. Modern Western democracies, especially England and the United States— that is, the so-called free societies—are characterized by legal and political arrangements that tend to place a very high value on individual liberty. This is exemplified by the Anglo-American criminal law. It is a system that affords many protections to persons accused of lawbreaking. And, of course, it affords complete protection against imprisonment in jails or similar institutions to people who are not accused of crime. Precisely because this system of social controls is so fine, so protective of individual rights, it leaves outside the scope of criminal law a wide range of behaviors that are socially disturbing. Thus, in Anglo-

American law, people have a right to be depressed or to talk crazy. At the same time, however, the so-called normal people in society do not want to put up with such behavior. Since they cannot control it one way, they will try to control it another way. That is how psychiatric sanctions have come into being and why they have become so popular: they satisfy a popular need for controlling certain behaviors that are not illegal but which "normal" people want controlled.

A brief review of the history of psychiatry may be in order here. The idea of regulating social behavior by psychiatry is only about three hundred years old. The first madhouses (mental hospitals or insane asylums) were built in France and Germany and then England around 1650. The people confined in these institutions were the homeless, orphans, poor people with infectious diseases, prostitutes, vagrants, and other such "miserables," as Victor Hugo would have put it. If we examine the development of these institutions, we see that the history of psychiatry is the opposite of the history of medicine. In medicine it was always obvious that there existed diseases that made people sick and killed them. Doctors, medicine, and hospitals came later. In psychiatry it was the other way around. First came the mental hospitals, then the mental diseases. In an important sense, mental diseases are social artifacts.

The first step in the history of psychiatry was the building of madhouses. That development created two populations, the keepers and the kept. There one has the role of power in psychiatry writ large. Who has the keys? Protesting the use of mental hospitalization in Russia, Solzhenitsyn declared, "The incarceration of free-thinking, healthy people in madhouses is spiritual murder, a variant of the gas chamber, and even more cruel." It seems to me that there is something terribly wrong with that statement. If incarcerating sane dissidents is worse than putting them in a gas chamber, how can it be good for mental patients? Should one not be even nicer to sick people than to healthy ones?

I think Solzhenitsyn is wrong, logically as well as morally. Nevertheless, his views reflect "enlightened" public opinion—namely, that it is acceptable to lock up crazy people in insane asylums, but it is not acceptable to lock up sane people in them. That is why it is now so popular a pastime in the West to protest the mental hospitalization of Soviet dissidents. Of course, the Russians say that they do not lock up "dissidents," they lock up "mental patients." In my opinion, the Russians are wrong, and the critics of Russian psychiatry are also wrong. The Russians are wrong because they have a political system that is evil from the ground up. Locking up dissidents in madhouses is just a part of it. The Western critics of Soviet psychiatry are wrong because they flatter themselves with selective indignation. They object to involuntary psychiatry in Russia, but not in the West. They object to incarcerating dissidents in mental hospitals, but do not object to incarcerating people behind the "iron curtains" within their own national borders.

A recent case of commitment in the United States, reported in the press, illustrates what is wrong with Solzhenitsyn's critique, and with the Western liberal critique in general, of Soviet psychiatry. A few years ago the Chicago police arrested a man named Robert Freedman for begging for dimes in front of a downtown bus station. He said, "Don't take me in, I am not drunk, I didn't know this [that is, begging] was a crime." When he opened the briefcase he carried with him, police found $24,098 in small bills. A few days later in court, a judge, who said he was protecting Freedman from possible bodily harm by thugs who might be after the cash he carried, committed Freedman to a mental hospital. Freedman did not suffer from a disease. Nevertheless, according to the newspapers, he "has seen half his life savings eaten away by hospital fees and doctors for treatment ordered by the court to keep him at a mental facility he fought to stay out of. The courts even ordered him to pay the fees for the lawyer who argued for his commitment." Three months after he was committed, Freedman was dead. Why did the judge commit him? Because, as he said after the commitment hearing, "I wonder what my decision would have been if he wasn't carrying $24,000 around. From the evidence, I decided that the man lacked good judgment. If he didn't have the $24,000 my interpretation of his judgment would have been different." That is what commitment is all about: deviant behavior and powerlessness on the one side; meddling, paternalism, and power on the other side. In the past, paternalism justified slavery, colonialism, male chauvinism. Now it justifies coercive psychiatry—and threatens to justify an increasing number of coercive medical interventions as well.

This, of course, is only one side of the story—the argument against psychiatric power. However, as John Stuart Mill so wisely observed, no one really understands a conflict unless he understands both sides of it. This warning is especially relevant to the controversy surrounding involuntary psychiatry—because the people who protest against the "abuses" of coercive psychiatry are often the ones most eager to preserve its "proper uses." That, I think, is something that cannot be done.

COERCIVE

As mentioned earlier, coercive psychiatric interventions are actually extralegal methods of social control. Their purpose is to take up the slack left by a criminal law "too protective" of individual liberty. But such a system of criminal law is emblematic of a people's devotion to the rule of law and the value of personal freedom. If and when a people decide to place a lower value on individual liberty, they usually revise their criminal statutes to reflect such a sentiment—for example, as the

Russians do in making emigration a criminal offense, and as we do by making use of certain drugs a criminal offense.

The very essence of the mental hygiene laws is thus to serve a purpose quite different from, indeed diametrically opposed to, the preservation of individual liberty. What is that purpose? It is to preserve and promote a common ideology or world view—that is, a shared sense of what is "normal"; it is also to preserve and protect the family from its excessively disruptive members—that is, from parents, children, or aged relatives who interfere with the well-being of the dominant members; and finally, it is to do so under medical and therapeutic, rather than penological or punitive, auspices—thus muting rather than polarizing conflicts in the family, on the job, in society as a whole. In short, just as individuals need "tranquilizers," so society, too, needs to have its conflicts defused and pacified. In past ages, organized religion fulfilled that task. Now psychiatry does. What we need to remember is that that task usually conflicts with the protection of individual dignity and liberty. Hence, it seems likely—indeed, certain—that not until we renounce or abolish involuntary psychiatric interventions will we develop mechanisms for defusing human conflicts that are less injurious to our most treasured traditional values than are the present methods of institutional psychiatry.

If we are honest with ourselves, we must recognize that neither the modern communist state nor the modern noncommunist state likes people who challenge its core values or whose behavior disrupts the traffic of everyday life. Faced with a choice between tolerating such behavior by looking the other way (or by some noncoercive method), and repressing it by means of psychiatric "treatment," every modern society opts for psychiatric sanctions. The very existence and attractiveness of psychiatric methods of social control fuel the engine of coercive psychiatry—its vocabulary, its imagery, and its specific techniques. Although there is no mental illness, modern society, to paraphrase Voltaire, finds it necessary to invent it. There is now no need for involuntary psychiatric interventions, but neither was there a need in the past for religious intolerance and persecution. Still, no one ever got a medal for being compassionate or tolerant—but many have received medals, and more, for persecuting people for their own good. The doctor who developed lobotomy—since prohibited both by the Soviets and the Vatican—received the Nobel Prize in medicine for it, the only such prize ever given for a so-called psychiatric discovery. Therein lies a lesson about the relations between psychiatry and power that people ignore at their own peril.

VI

What Are
the Value Conflicts
and Assumptions?

When writers are trying to convince you of their point of view, they are shrewd. They present reasons that are consistent with their positions. That is why, at first glance, most arguments "make sense." The visible structure looks good. But the reasons that are *stated* are not the only beliefs that the writer is using to prove or support her opinion. There are hidden or unstated thoughts that may be at least as significant in understanding her argument. Let's examine the importance of these unstated beliefs by considering the following brief argument.

> The government should prohibit the manufacture and sale of cigarettes. More and more evidence has demonstrated that smoking has harmful effects on the health of both the smoker and those exposed to smoking.

The reason—at first glance—supports the conclusion. If the government wants to prohibit a product, it makes sense that it should provide evidence that the product is bad. But it is also possible that the reason given can be true and yet *not necessarily* support the conclusion. What if you believe that it is the individual's responsibility to take care of his own welfare, not the collective responsibility of government. If so, from your perspective, the reason no longer supports the conclusion. This reasoning is convincing to you only if you agree with certain unstated beliefs that the writer has taken for granted. In this case, the belief taken for granted is that collective responsibility is more desirable than individual responsibility when an individual's welfare is threatened.

In all arguments, there will be certain beliefs taken for granted by the writer. Typically, these beliefs will not be stated. You will have to find them by reading between the lines. These beliefs are important invisible links in the reasoning structure, the glue that holds the entire argument together. Until you supply these links, you cannot truly understand the argument.

Your task is similar in many ways to having to reproduce a magic trick without having seen how the magician did the trick. You see the handkerchief go into the hat and the rabbit come out, but you are not aware of the magician's hidden maneuvers. To understand the trick, you must discover these maneuvers. Likewise, in arguments, you must discover the hidden maneuvers, which in actuality are unstated beliefs. We shall refer to these unstated beliefs as *assumptions*. To fully understand an argument, you must identify the assumptions.

Assumptions are

1. hidden or unstated (in most cases),
2. taken for granted,
3. influential in determining the conclusion,
4. necessary, if the reasoning is to make sense, and
5. potentially deceptive.

This chapter and the next one will show you how to discover assumptions. We will focus on one kind of assumption in this chapter—value assumptions.

◊ *Critical Question:* **What are the value conflicts and assumptions?**

General Guide for Identifying Assumptions

When you seek assumptions, where and how should you look? In any book or article there are numerous assumptions. Fortunately, you need to be concerned about relatively few. As you remember, the visible structure of an argument is contained in reasons and conclusions. Thus, you are interested only in assumptions that affect the quality of this structure. You can restrict your search for assumptions, therefore, to the structure you have already learned how to identify. **Look for assumptions in the move from reasons to conclusions!**

Notice that the search for assumptions is focused on the same place that you are looking for ambiguity. Can you now see the importance of identifying structure initially? If you waited to find reasons and conclusions until later in your thought sequence, you would be wasting a lot of time since you wouldn't have any guidelines for knowing which sentences or paragraphs are more important than others. We will give you several hints on this subject in the next chapter.

Value Conflicts and Assumptions

Why is it that some very reasonable people charge that abortion is murder, while other equally reasonable observers see abortion as humane? Have you ever wondered why every President, regardless of his political beliefs, eventually gets involved in a dispute with the press over publication of government information that he would prefer not to share? How can some highly intelligent observers attack the publication of sexually explicit magazines and others defend their publication as the ultimate test of our Bill of Rights?

The primary answer to all these questions is the existence of value conflicts or different frames of reference. For ethical or prescriptive arguments, an individual's values influence the reasons he provides and, consequently, his conclusion. Value assumptions—beliefs about which values are most important—are, therefore, very important assumptions for such arguments. You should make it a habit to find out whether the value assumptions on which reasons are based are consistent with your own value assumptions before accepting or rejecting a conclusion.

Some of the most fundamental assumptions are those relating to value priorities. The rest of this chapter is devoted to increasing your awareness of the role played by value conflicts in determining a person's opinions or conclusions. This awareness will help you to locate and evaluate this important type of assumption.

Discovering Values

Before you can discover the importance of values in shaping conclusions, you must have some understanding of what a value is. Values may be objects, experiences, actions, or ideas that someone thinks are worthwhile. You will find, however, that it is the importance one assigns to abstract *ideas*, above all, that has the major influence on one's choices and behavior. Usually objects, experiences, and actions are desired because of some idea we value. For example, we may choose to do things that provide us with contacts with important people. We probably value "important people" because we value "status." When we use the word *value* in this chapter, we will be referring to an idea representing what someone thinks is important and will strive to achieve.

To better familiarize yourself with values, write down some of your own values. Try to avoid writing down the names of people, tangible objects, or actions. Marlon Brando, pizza, and playing tennis may be important to you, but it is the importance you assign to ideas that most influences your choices and behavior concerning controversial public issues. Your willingness to argue for or against capital punishment, for instance, is strongly related to the importance you assign to the sanctity of human life—an abstract idea. The sanctity of human life is a value that affects our opinions about war, abortion, drug usage, and mercy killing. As you create your list of values, focus on those that are so significant that they affect your opinions and behavior in many ways.

Did you have problems making your list? We can suggest two further aids that may help. First, another definition! Values are *standards of conduct* that we endorse and expect people to meet. When we expect our political representatives to "tell the truth," we are indicating to them and to ourselves that honesty is one of our most cherished values. Ask yourself what you expect your friends to be like. What standards of conduct would you want your children to develop? Answers to these questions should help you enlarge your understanding of values.

When you are thinking about standards of conduct as a means of discovering values, recognize that certain conduct has a more significant effect on your life than does other behavior. Certain values have a larger personal and social impact than others. Politeness, for instance, is a standard of conduct and a value, but it does not have the major impact on our lives that a value such as competition has. The point here is that certain values have greater consequences than others. Thus, you will usually want to focus on the values that most affect our behavior.

Now let us give you an aid for identifying values—a list of some commonly held values. Every value on our list may be an attractive candidate for your list. Thus, after you look at our list, pause for a moment and choose those values that are most important to you. They will be those values that most often play a role in shaping your opinions and behavior.

COMMON VALUES

adventure	wisdom	excellence
novelty	collective choice	flexibility
equality of opportunity	obedience to authority	spontaneity
equality of condition	honesty	patriotism
ambition	comfort	justice
courage	peace	tolerance
generosity	security	self-control
independence	freedom of speech	competition
rationality	harmony	cooperation
order	creativity	productivity

From Values to Value Assumptions

To identify value assumptions, we must go beyond a simple listing of values. Many of your values are shared by others. Wouldn't almost anyone claim that flexibility, cooperation, and honesty are desirable? Since many values are shared, values by themselves are not a powerful guide to understanding. What leads you to answer a prescriptive question differently from someone else is the relative intensity with which each of you holds specific values.

Differences in intensity of allegiance to particular values can easily be seen by thinking about responses to controversies when pairs of values collide or conflict. While it is not very enlightening to discover that most people value both competition and cooperation, we do gain a more complete understanding of prescriptive choices as we discover who *prefers* competition to cooperation when the two values conflict.

For example, parents disagree about the desirability of placing especially talented students in separate classes where their learning can be accelerated. One basis for this disagreement is the different importance that parents may attribute to competition and cooperation. If a parent would rather see competition (that is, an identifiable struggle among students with different intellectual capacities) increased rather than see cooperation encouraged, then this parent is likely to approve of the establishment of separate classes for talented students. One factor that would divide parents on this issue is their differing preferences concerning the importance of competition and cooperation.

A writer's preferences for particular values are often unstated, but they will have a major impact on her conclusion and on how she chooses to defend it. These unstated assertions about value priorities function as *value assumptions*. Recognition of relative support for conflicting values or sets of values provides you with both an improved understanding of what you are reading and a basis for eventual evaluation of prescriptive arguments.

When a writer takes a stand on controversial prescriptive issues, he is usually depreciating one commonly shared value while upholding another. For example, when someone advocates the required licensing of prospective parents, collective responsibility is being treated as more important than individual responsibility. So when you look for value assumptions, look for an indication of value preferences. Ask yourself what values are being upheld by this position and what values are being depreciated.

When you have found a person's value preference in a particular argument, you should not expect that same person to have the same value priority when discussing a different controversy. A person does not have the same value priorities without regard to the issue being discussed. In Chapter XIV you will learn about how people often select their value assumptions; you will realize that it is highly unlikely that a person would maintain a rigid set of value assumptions that he would apply to every controversy.

Typical Value Conflicts

If you are aware of typical value conflicts, you can more quickly recognize the assumptions being made by a writer when she reaches a particular conclusion. We have listed some of the more common value conflicts that occur in ethical issues and have provided you with examples of controversies in which these value conflicts are likely to be evident. We anticipate that you can use this list as a starting point when you are trying to identify important value assumptions.

TYPICAL VALUE CONFLICTS AND SAMPLE CONTROVERSIES

1. loyalty—honesty	1. Should you tell your parents about your sister's drug habit?
2. competition—cooperation	2. Do you support the grading system?
3. freedom of press—national security	3. Is it wise to hold weekly Presidential press conferences?
4. equality—individualism	4. Are racial quotas for employment fair?
5. order—freedom of speech	5. Should we imprison those with radical ideas?
6. security—excitement	6. Should you choose a dangerous profession?
7. generosity—material success	7. Is it desirable to give financial help to a beggar?
8. rationality—spontaneity	8. Should you check the odds before placing a bet?
9. tradition—novelty	9. Should divorces be easily available?

As you identify value conflicts, you will often find that there are several value conflicts that seem important in shaping conclusions with respect to particular controversies. It is arbitrary to choose one particular value conflict as the only one at issue. When evaluating a controversy, try to find several value conflicts, as a check on yourself. Some controversies will have one primary value conflict; others may have several.

Take another look at number 7 in the preceding list. It is quite possible that value conflicts besides that between generosity and material success affect your decision about whether to give financial help to a beggar. For instance, all the following value conflicts may affect a person's willingness to help a beggar:

1. individualism—collective responsibility
2. competition—cooperation
3. efficiency—social stability

By identifying as many of the relevant value assumptions as possible, you have a better chance of not missing any of the important dimensions of the argument. However, you may have no way of knowing which value assumptions are actually responsible for the author's conclusion.

The Writer's Background as a Clue to Value Assumptions

It has already been suggested that a good starting point in finding value assumptions is to check the background of the author. Find out as much as you can about the value preferences usually held by a person like the writer. Is he a big-businessman, a union leader, a Republican Party official, a doctor, or an apartment tenant? What interests does such a person naturally wish to protect? There's certainly nothing inherently wrong with pursuing self-interest, but such pursuits often limit the value assumptions a particular writer will tolerate. For example, it's highly unlikely that the president of a major automobile firm would place a high value on efficiency when a preference for efficiency rather than stability would lead to his losing his job. Consequently, you as a critical reader can often quickly discover value preferences by thinking about the probable assumptions made by a person like the writer.

One caution is important. It isn't necessarily true that, because a writer is a member of a group, she shares the particular value assumptions of the group. It would be mistaken to presume that every individual who belongs to a given group thinks identically. We all know that businessmen, farmers, and firemen sometimes disagree among themselves when discussing particular controversies. Investigating the writer's background as a clue to her value assumptions is only a clue, and like other clues it can be misleading unless it is used with care.

Consequences as a Clue to Value Assumptions

In prescriptive arguments, each position with respect to an issue leads to different consequences or outcomes when the position is acted upon. Each of the potential consequences will have a certain likelihood of occurring, and each will also have some level of desirability or undesirability. How desirable a consequence is will depend on a writer's or reader's personal value preferences. The desirability of the conclusions in such cases will be dictated by the probability of the potential consequences and the importance attached to them. Thus, an important means of determining an individual's value assumptions is to examine the reasons given in support of a conclusion and then to determine what value preferences would lead to these reasons being judged as more desirable than reasons that might have been offered on the other side of the issue. Let's take a look at a concrete example.

ARGUMENT: *Nuclear power plants should not be built because they will pollute our environment.*

The reason provided here is a rather specific potential consequence of building nuclear plants. This writer clearly sees environmental pollution as very undesirable. Why does this consequence carry so much weight in this person's thinking? What more general value does preventing pollution help achieve? Probably conservation, or perhaps naturalness. Someone else might stress a different consequence in this argument, such as the effect on the supply of electricity to consumers. Why? Probably because he values efficiency very highly. Thus, this reason supports the conclusion *if* a value assumption is made that conservation is more important than efficiency.

Note that the *magnitude* of a consequence may have a major impact on value preferences. One may value conservation over efficiency only when efficiency may cause "significant" damage to the environment. And one may value free enterprise over economic security only as long as unemployment stays below a given level.

One important means of determining value assumptions, then, is to ask the question, Why do the particular consequences or outcomes presented as reasons seem so desirable to the writer or speaker?

REMEMBER: When you identify *value assumptions*, you should always state *value preferences*. With controversial topics, stating value assumptions in this way will be a continual reminder both of what the writer is *giving up* and of what she is gaining.

More Hints for Finding Value Assumptions

Many social controversies share important characteristics; they are thus *analogous* to one another. The value preferences implicit in a certain controversy can sometimes be discovered by searching for analogous elements in other social controversies. Do any common characteristics have their origin in a similar value conflict?

Let's ask, for instance, how a particular controversy is similar to other controversies, and see whether the answer gives us a clue to an important value assumption.

> Should the government require car manufacturers to include air bags in automobiles?

What are the important characteristics of this controversy? The controversy, more generally, asks whether collective groups, such as the government, should intervene in people's lives to help them protect themselves. Such an intervention is analogous to banning cigarette advertising, requiring motorcycle riders to wear helmets, and banning boxing. Once you have recognized the similarity of these issues, you should be able to see how certain values will dictate individuals' positions on them. Someone who believes that the government should require air bags in cars is also likely to believe that the government should ban cigarette advertising. Why? Becaue he values collective responsibility and public safety more than individual responsibility.

See if you can name a controversy analogous to the following:

> Should it be legal for newspaper and television reporters to refuse to reveal their confidential sources?

How did you do? We thought of the question of whether psychiatrists should be allowed to refuse to testify about their patients in murder trials. Whatever different examples you thought of, our guess is that your thinking made you aware of some important values, such as privacy, the public's right to know, or public safety. Awareness of value conflicts is a necessary step toward determining value assumptions.

Another useful technique for generating value conflicts is to *reverse role-play*. Ask the question, What do those people who would take a different position from the writer's care about? When someone argues that we should not use monkeys in experimental research, you should ask yourself, If I wanted to defend the use of monkeys, what would I be concerned about? Remember, when someone takes a position on a controversial topic, she will be revealing a value *preference*. Your knowledge of that preference will help you to decide whether or not to agree with her conclusion.

Finding Value Assumptions on Your Own

Let's work on an example together to help you become more comfortable with finding value assumptions.

> A nearby college campus is trying to decide whether the campus police should be permitted to carry weapons. Passions run high on both sides

of the debate. An expert on crime prevention testifies that weapons act as a preventive measure. Potential criminals know that the risk of harm to themselves is greater if there are armed officers in the vicinity of the planned criminal act. A professor responds that police should not be carrying weapons on a college campus, for the use of weapons is inconsistent with the problem solving by rational discussion that universities teach.

The structure of the two positions is outlined here for you:

CONCLUSION 1: *Campus police should be permitted to carry weapons.*

REASON: *Police with weapons are more effective in preventing crime than are unarmed officers.*

CONCLUSION 2: *Campus police should not carry weapons.*

REASON: *Allowing police to carry weapons on a college campus is inconsistent with rational discussion as a means of solving campus problems.*

Try looking for the value conflicts that lie at the root of the disagreement. Imagine that you have become involved in that debate. Which of the values you listed as your own would play an important role in determining how you feel?

Let us suggest one value conflict that strikes us as important regarding this issue. Note that the expert on crime prevention stresses the potential negative consequence of not apprehending criminals. Why? Police see it as their responsibility to preserve the order created by our legal system. That legal order is the special way in which order is defined in the value conflict stimulated by this controversy. Guns stop criminals more definitely than words do. Hence, police tend to argue for their need to be armed.

Those who resist the arming of campus police see a college campus as one environment in which rationality should serve as the means for resolving disputes. A gun in the hands of a campus policeman is an insult to their faith in the use of reason, since you cannot reason with a gun.

Thus a major value conflict here is *order vs. rationality*; when someone argues for arming campus police, she is making a value assumption that, in this situation, order is more important than rationality. Note that the supporters of arming campus police are not in favor of irrationality, nor are their opponents in favor of disorder. When you are making a decision, however, you often must choose between two values, each of which is important to you. In this instance, the supporters of arming the campus police simply rank order higher than encouragement of rationality as a means of conflict resolution.

Let's complete one more example together.

Students should obey a dress code that includes uniforms, shoe restrictions, and hair length. In such an educational setting, teachers can teach and students can learn. Valuable time and energy will not be wasted on the discipline problems that arise in the absence of a rigid dress code.

Let's first outline the structure of the argument.

CONCLUSION: *Students should obey a rigid dress code.* Ordered, freedom of ind—

REASON: *Discipline problems would be reduced by obedience to such a code.*

What value assumption do you think would result in someone's support for a rigid dress code for the schools? Look back at the table on page 57. Would any of the sample value conflicts affect one's reaction to school dress codes and the use of the above reasoning? Try to explain how a preference for educational excellence over individual self-expression might affect your reaction to this controversy.

Identifying value assumptions is not only necessary to understand why someone makes a particular claim, but it will also help you relate the various conclusions arrived at by the same individual. As we try to understand one another, it is sometimes helpful to recognize patterns in our behavior. One key to patterns of human behavior is an appreciation of value conflicts. Although you cannot be sure, it is a good first guess to predict that those who prefer to see campus police with weapons will also favor a hard-line approach to negotiations with the Soviet Union, spanking as a form of discipline, and tougher jail sentences for juvenile delinquents.

Practice Exercises

◊ *Critical Question:* **What are the value conflicts and assumptions?**

Identify the value conflicts that could lead to agreement or disagreement with the following points of view, then identify the value priorities assumed by the writer.

Passage 1

Some members of our society receive outrageous sums of money each year. Athletes, entertainers, and executives receive incomes that most of us can hardly imagine. At the same time, in the same country, other people are unable to heat their homes, afford nutritious meals, or fi-

Equality

nance an automobile. No one should be allowed to make a salary that is 100 times larger than that of the average person.

Passage 2

We rarely tell young people the truth about marriage. The truth is that marriage is a terrible habit. It ruins voluntary love. Exciting romances are changed into dull marriages. What was a love affair becomes a grinding, limiting contract.

Passage 3

For most people, college is a waste of time and money. One does not need schools to learn. If you go to college to make it possible to earn more money, you have been had. More than half of those who earn more than $15,000 never received a college diploma. What you do learn in college is rarely useful on the job. Most of you would be better off saving part of the money you earn while your naïve friends are in college.

--- **SAMPLE RESPONSES** ---

Passage 1

CONCLUSION: *No one should make more than 100 times the salary of the average worker.*

REASON: *The gap between rich and poor is preventing some Americans from having basic necessities.*

One value conflict that would cause readers to disagree is that between equal opportunity and equality of condition. The argument depends on the importance of everyone's having the basic necessities. The existence of huge incomes limits the amount of money left over for others to buy those necessities. Hence those who value equality of condition more than equality of opportunity may well argue that regardless of the similar opportunities available to all workers, each of us should be guaranteed a basic level of goods and services.

Passage 2

CONCLUSION: *Marriage should be discouraged.*

REASONS: *1. Love is no longer voluntary when one marries.* Security +
          2. Marriage is relatively dull and repetitive. variety

One value conflict is between security and variety. The author apparently prefers variety to security. He criticizes marriage as dull and habitual. Those who value security more than variety may well disagree with the author.

Passage 3

CONCLUSION: *Most young people should not attend college.*

REASONS: *1. Many of those who make a lot of money never attended college.*
2. College does not generally teach job-related skills.

A value assumption is that materialistic achievement is more important than wisdom. Notice that the consequence stressed by the author is the impact of college on future income. She addresses none of the other purposes one might have for attending college. If one valued wisdom more than monetary accumulation, one might well reject the reasoning suggested in this passage.

Passage 4 (Self-Examination)

The United States must maintain large numbers of troops to protect its interests in different parts of the world. The forces must be composed of young people because only they are physically and mentally able to risk their lives and kill if necessary. A draft, unlike a voluntary system, underlines a sense of national identity and commitment. We need a lottery to choose those who will be drafted so that luck, rather than lack of skill or income, determines who our soldiers will be. A voluntary military creates the very real possibility that dangerous personality types will be given power over our armaments and future.

VII

What Are the Definitional and Descriptive Assumptions?

You should now be able to identify value assumptions—very important hidden links in prescriptive arguments. When you find value assumptions, you know pretty well what a writer wants the world to be like—what ideas he thinks are most important to strive for. But you do not know what he *believes is true* about what the world was, is, or will be like, except for the little bit you know from his visible reasoning. Yet his visible reasoning depends on these beliefs, as well as upon his values. Such unstated beliefs are descriptive assumptions, and they are essential hidden links in an argument.

Besides having underlying value preferences and beliefs, many arguments are based on unstated definitions of key terms. The reasoning only makes sense given the writer's particular choice of definitions; other definitional choices would invalidate the reasoning.

This chapter focuses on the identification of descriptive and definitional assumptions.

◊   *Critical Question:* **What are the definitional and descriptive assumptions?**

Clarifying Definitional and Descriptive Assumptions

Let us use a self-test to illustrate more clearly what we mean by descriptive and definitional assumptions, and also to give you a better idea of your own understanding of such assumptions. Try to locate an assumption in the following quote:

> You will learn a lot from Professor Starr. His students all rave about his lectures.

Could you do it? Compare your answers with ours. We will first provide the structure of the argument, then state assumptions.

CONCLUSION: You will learn a lot from Professor Starr.

REASON: His students all rave about his lectures.

ASSUMPTION 1: *Student's comments are a good indicator of lecture quality.* If students are not capable of judging lecture quality, then the reason given is not supportive of the conclusion.

ASSUMPTION 2: *To learn a lot means to absorb material from a lecture.* (Sponge-model thinking, right?) If you define "learn a lot" as developing thinking skills, then the amount of raving about lectures may be irrelevant. This assumption is thus a definitional assumption. The conclusion follows the reason only if a certain definition of *learn* is assumed.

Note that there are other hidden assumptions in this argument. For example, you should not be convinced by this reasoning unless you believe that the qualities others look for in lectures are the same qualities you look for. Should you eat at a restaurant because many of your friends rave about it? Wouldn't you want to know why they rave about it?

Remember: Many arguments will contain multiple assumptions.

Clues for Locating Assumptions

Your job in finding assumptions is to reconstruct the reasoning by filling in the missing gaps. That is, you want to provide beliefs that help the writer's reasoning "make sense." Once you have a picture of the entire argument, both the visible and the invisible parts, you will be in a much better position to determine its strengths and weaknesses.

How does one go about finding these important missing links? It requires hard work, imagination, and creativity. Finding important assumptions is a difficult task.

You have been introduced to three types of assumptions—value, definitional, and descriptive. We can give you a few clues that will make your search for assumptions rewarding.

Keep thinking about the conclusion! Why are you looking for assumptions in the first place? You are looking because you want to be able to judge the worth of the conclusion. You are looking for what the writer would have had to believe in order to link the reasons and conclusion together. As you look for assumptions, keep asking yourself, How does that reason support the conclusion? Ask, If the reason is true, what else must be true for the conclusion to follow? It is also useful to ask, Is there any way the reason could be true but the conclusion false?

Identify with the writer. Locating someone's assumptions is often made easier by imagining that you were asked to defend the conclusion. If you can, crawl into the skin of a person who would reach such a conclusion. Discover the background of the writer. Whether the person whose conclusion you are evaluating is a corporate executive, a communist, a labor leader, a boxing promoter, or a judge, try to play the role of such a person and plan in your mind what he would be thinking as he moved toward the conclusion. When an executive for a coal company argues that strip mining does not significantly harm the beauty of our natural environment, he has probably begun with a belief that strip mining is beneficial to our nation. Thus, he may assume a definition of beauty that would be consistent with his arguments, while other definitions of beauty would lead to a condemnation of strip mining.

Identify with the opposition. If you are unable to locate assumptions by taking the role of the speaker or writer, try to reverse roles. Ask yourself why anyone might disagree with the conclusion. What type of reasoning would prompt someone to disagree with the conclusion you are evaluating? If you can play the role of a person who would not accept the conclusion, you can more readily see assumptions in the original structure.

Recognize the potential existence of other means of attaining the advantages referred to in the reasons. Frequently, a conclusion is supported by reasons that indicate the various advantages of acting on the author's conclusion. When there are many ways to reach the same advantages, one important assumption linking the reasons to the conclusion is that the best way to attain the advantages is through the author's conclusion.

Let's try this technique with one brief example. Many counselors would argue that a college freshman should be allowed to choose her own courses without any restrictions from parents or college personnel because it facilitates the growth of personal responsibility. But aren't there many ways to encourage the growth of personal responsibility? Might not some of these alternatives have less serious disadvantages than those that could result when a freshman makes erroneous judgments about which courses would be in her best long-term interest? For example, the development of personal responsibility is furthered by requiring a student to make a substantial financial contribution to the cost of her education. Thus, those who argue that it is desirable to permit college freshmen to make their own course choices because such an opportunity encourages personal responsibility are assuming that there are not less risky alternatives for accomplishing a similar goal.

Learn more about issues. The more familiar you are with all sides of a topic, the more easily you will be able to locate assumptions. Get as much information about the issues you care about as you can.

Searching for Definitional and Descriptive Assumptions

The previous section provided you with some general clues for finding all three types of assumptions. In addition to these general clues, there are a few more specific questions you can ask yourself in order to find definitional and descriptive assumptions.

First, ask yourself the following questions: Are there key terms in the controversy as stated, in the conclusion, or in the reasons that have multiple potential meanings? Will the writer's reasoning make sense only if a particular meaning is supplied? Look especially for key nouns and adjectives. We have italicized key words in the following controversies. See if you can determine what definitional assumptions might have to be made in order to respond to these controversies.

Is *psychotherapy effective*?

Should the *poor* receive increased welfare payments?

Are *churches dying* in America?

Was President Truman a *conservative* president?

Does *jogging* improve one's *mental health*?

Did you come up with something like the following for the last question? *Jogging* could be defined as accumulating 60 miles per week at a rapid pace or, alternatively, as totaling 15 miles per week at a slow pace. Maybe jogging only improves mental health given one of these two definitions.

The next question you should ask is, What else does the writer have to believe about what is true of the past, the present, or the future in order for his reasoning to make sense? The answer to this question will be a descriptive assumption. For example, when an individual argues that capital punishment is needed because it will be an effective crime deterrent, she must also believe that people think about the consequences prior to engaging in criminal acts. This belief is a descriptive assumption.

An Illustration of Definitional and Descriptive Assumptions

Let's look at an argument against cloning and see whether we can identify both definitional and descriptive assumptions.

Cloning is a process whereby children can be produced using only one parent. The consequences of human cloning are almost impossible to imagine. If there were widespread human cloning, our society would be changed beyond recognition. How could the family continue to exist if there were no longer a link between reproduction and the sexual sharing of the marriage partners? No longer would we have the diversity of humans that makes all our lives so rich. Someone might create communities where people all looked and behaved the same.

Think of the power possessed by those who would decide who gets cloned. Would they prefer opera singers to jazz pianists, baseball players to gardeners, or dancers to jockeys? Does the history of the species suggest that we can trust other citizens to have such power? To succeed as a species we need to be able to adapt to changes. It's quite possible that our ability to adapt is dependent on diversity in our gene pool. Cloning might destroy that diversity in our efforts to improve the quality of our species.

The structure of the argument appears to be the following:

CONCLUSION: *Cloning should be discouraged.*

REASONS: *1. Families would be destroyed if there were no longer a necessary link between sexual intimacy and reproduction.*
    2. There would be too much power in the hands of the cloners.
    3. Cloning would reduce the human diversity needed for adaption to unknown futures.

Now let's see if any definitional or descriptive assumptions can be found in the argument. Remember to keep the conclusion in focus as you look. Ask yourself, What must be true for the reasons to be true? Why do these reasons support the conclusion? Are there any key words in the reasons that must be carefully defined before they are analyzed? Look at the first reason. How does the author define families? Would all forms of family life be destroyed simply because marriage partners no longer needed their spouses for purposes of reproduction? Apparently, the author's concept of family is based on the necessary role of human reproduction. *Families are those institutions required for such reproduction.* That's a definitional assumption that the author would like you to accept. This assumption is necessary for one of the reasons to make sense.

Another assumption is required for the second reason to lead to the conclusion. If someone is afraid of giving a group of scientists extensive power, what beliefs would they have about what the world was, is, or will be like? They would surely not have confidence that humans have demonstrated their ability to control potentially dangerous processes like cloning. For the second reason to prove that cloning should be discouraged, the descriptive assumption that *humans are unlikely to control potentially dangerous scientific knowledge responsibly* must be made. With that assumption the conclusion makes more sense. The second reason is thereby linked to the conclusion that cloning should be discouraged.

Note also that since this is a prescriptive argument, important value assumptions will underlie the reasoning. For example, can you see how a preference for tradition and naturalness over technological and scientific development would lead to this type of reasoning?

What is the author concerned about preserving? Try role-playing in reverse. What would someone who disagreed with this position care about? What are the advantages of cloning? Your answers to these questions should lead you to the essay's value preferences.

Avoiding Analysis of Trivial Assumptions

Authors take for granted certain self-evident things that we should not concern ourselves about. You will want to devote your energy to evaluating important assumptions, so we want to warn you about some potential trivial assumptions.

You as a reader can assume that the writer believes his reasons are true. You may want to attack the reasons as insufficient, but it is trivial to point out the writer's assumption that they are true.

Another type of trivial assumption concerns the reasoning structure. You may be tempted to state that the writer believes that the reason and conclusion are logically related. Right—but trivial. What is important is *how* they are logically related. It is also trivial to point out that an argument assumes that we can understand the logic, that we can understand the terminology, or that we have the appropriate background knowledge.

Avoid spending time on analyzing trivial assumptions. Your search for assumptions will be most rewarding when you locate hidden, debatable missing links.

Quality of Assumptions as a Legitimate Filter

After you have located assumptions, you must make an attempt to determine whether the assumptions make sense. You have not criticized a conclusion effectively simply because you have located assumptions in the reasoning. All of us assume many things when we communicate. Making assumptions is normal when we speak or write.

It is the quality of the assumptions that affects whether we should agree with a line of reasoning. If you have some basis for doubting the appropriateness of an assumption, then it is fair to reject the reason or conclusion that was propped up by that assumption. Don't be shy about disagreeing with an author once you have identified her shaky assumptions. It is the writer's responsibility to justify any assumptions about which you have some doubt; if she doesn't do that satisfactorily, then you should refuse to accept her conclusions.

One final note concerning locating assumptions. In this chapter we have not discussed assumptions that fill in the gaps in arguments that rely heavily on statistical evidence. We make many assumptions when we use evidence to support conclusions. You will directly confront these assumptions as you read Chapters VIII through X. When you have completed them, you should be sensitive to many potential missing links in reasoning with evidence.

Practice Exercises

◊ *Critical Question:* **What are the definitional and descriptive assumptions?**

For each of the three passages, locate important assumptions made by the author. Remember first to determine the conclusion and the reasons.

Passage 1

Reverence for human life is basic to the moral foundation of a just society. That is why the abolition of the death penalty is a major step in society's long road to civilization. More than 70 nations have already recognized the immorality of the death penalty by abolishing it.

Executions offer few benefits to society, and instead present embarrassing evidence that our lust for vengeance often overpowers our humanity. Executions do not act as a deterrent to potential murders. Studies that have compared the murder rates in communities that do and do not have the death penalty have found no differences. Such evidence is not surprising: Murder is an irrational act, often an act of passion.

Because the death penalty is absolute and irrevocable, it violates our ideal of rehabilitation. As long as we are capable of making mistakes in criminal trials (and we have made many), we will be executing victims, not criminals.

Passage 2

Juvenile delinquents rarely have parents who establish clear rules and enforce them. Books on child rearing have increasingly stressed the need for a permissive, liberal home environment. At the same time, juvenile delinquency rates have been rising sharply. Encouraging stricter discipline at home, rather than more aggressive law enforcement, offers the key to reducing the growth of juvenile delinquency.

Passage 3

My answer to genocide, quite simply, is eight black kids—and another baby on the way.

I guess it is just that "slave/master" complex white folks have. For years they told us where to sit, where to eat, and where to live. First the white man tells me to sit at the back of the bus. Now it looks like he wants me to sleep under the bed. Back in the days of slavery, black folks couldn't grow kids fast enough for whites to harvest. Now that we've got a little taste of power, white folks want us to call a moratorium on having babies.

Of course, I could never participate in birth control, because I'm against doing anything that goes against Nature. That's why I've changed my eating habits so drastically over the years and have become a vegetarian. And birth control is definitely against Nature. Can you believe that human beings are the only creatures who would ever consider developing birth-control pills? You mention contraception to a gorilla, and he will tear your head off.[1]

SAMPLE RESPONSES

In presenting assumptions for the following arguments, we will list only *some* of the assumptions being made—those which we believe to be among the most significant.

Passage 1

CONCLUSION: *We must abolish the death penalty.*

REASONS: 1. *Abolishing the death penalty reflects reverence for human life.*
2. *Many other nations have abolished the death penalty.*
3. *Executions reflect a societal attitude of vengeance, rather than humaneness.*
4. *Executions do not deter murder.*
5. *The death penalty is irrevocable.*

---

[1]Adapted from Dick Gregory, "My Answer to Genocide," *Ebony* (October 1971), 66.

To support the conclusion, the first reason requires the definitional assumption that *reverence for human life is best shown by society's refraining from making a choice to take a life.* If one defined reverence for human life as society's decreeing that those who take another's life must forfeit their own, then capital punishment is more reasonable.

In order for the second reason to support the conclusion, the reasoning must assume that *our country is highly similar in its beliefs, attitudes, and values to these other countries.* If there are major differences among these countries and ours—in attitudes toward personal responsibility and punishment, for example—then the position of these other countries toward capital punishment may not be very relevant. (As critical thinkers, we should ask, Why have these countries rejected capital punishment?)

The fourth reason relies upon evidence comparing murder rates among communities. Thus, to accept the reason as true, one must assume that the *comparisons between communities allowed sufficient time for the effects of executions to occur.* Also, the credibility of the reasoning requires the assumption that *the executions have been highly publicized in these comparison communities.*

When the author argues in the fourth reason that executions do not deter murders because murders are acts of passion, he assumes *that passion is such an intense emotion that rational processes are totally impaired.* But perhaps, even in moments of passion, potential murderers may have *some* awareness of possible consequences.

An important assumption for linking the fifth reason to the conclusion is that *our legal system will not develop safeguards against the possibility of executing innocent victims,* such as permitting a death penalty sentence only under very special evidential conditions.

We have listed some assumptions; you can determine others by carefully looking for gaps in the reasoning.

Passage 2

CONCLUSION: *The key to reducing juvenile delinquency is to encourage stricter discipline at home.*

REASONS: 1. *Juvenile delinquents rarely have parents who establish clear rules and enforce them.*
2. *An increased emphasis in popular books on permissive, liberal home environments has occurred at the same time as juvenile delinquency rates have risen.*

For the first reason to support the conclusion, it must be assumed that, *because there is an association between parental discipline and delinquency, one causes the other.* Perhaps lax parenting is caused by parents who have a basic uncaring attitude. The linkage between the second reason and the conclusion requires the assumption that, *because two things have occurred simultaneously, one has caused the other.* After all, television violence may also have increased during the same period.

Note that there is a value preference underlying the entire reasoning—the belief that tradition and family are more important values to uphold than rule by law. If one valued rule by law more strongly, then one would be more likely to argue for increasing penalties for juvenile delinquency than for changing the home environment.

Passage 3

Conclusion: *Birth control is wrong.*

Reasons: *1. Birth control is just another attempt by the white folks to exercise their "slave/master" complex and keep the blacks from growing in power.*
2. Birth control goes against Nature.

What does the writer take for granted in order for the first reason to be true?

> *a. Blacks will use birth-control methods to a greater extent than will whites. (If he believed that whites would use birth-control procedures more than blacks, then the end result of birth-control measures would be an increase in the black population relative to the white population.)*
> *b. The number of blacks is an important determinant of the power of blacks.*

What must the writer take for granted in order for the first reason to support the conclusion?

> *a. Racial power considerations are more important than the environmental resource considerations that are affected by population growth.*

What does the writer take for granted in relating the second reason to the conclusion?

> *a. Mankind should not attempt to control its fate through artificial or technological means; rather, we should accept the natural order.*

Passage 4 (Self-Examination): Complex Passage

Television[2]

WALTER ISAACSON

Television is, by its very nature, a harmful, narcotic influence. Irrespective of the content of its shows, the very act of watching TV tends

[2]Reprinted by permission of the Putnam Publishing Group from PRO AND CON by Walter Isaacson. Copyright 1983 © by Walter Isaacson.

to numb the brain, dull creativity, alienate personalities, suppress imagination, and lull us into a zombie existence. Couple this inherent destructiveness of the medium with the actual content of 99 percent of the boob tube's wasteland, and it becomes clear that before our very eyes, but with us hardly noticing it, TV is corroding society.

No doubt a thin argument can be made for occasional TV viewing, watching a show for a specific piece of information. That is not, however, what is at question. The average U.S. household has a set on almost seven hours a day. Most people watch more than thirty hours per week. By the time a person graduates from high school, he or she will have watched 18,000 hours of TV and spent only 12,000 hours at school. People spend more time watching TV than talking, reading, or playing. Next to sleeping, it is the most common activity (or lack of activity) in America today.

The basic problem is TV's effect on the brain: quite simply, it produces a stupor. This is not because the shows are generally boring, but because of something inherent in the way video images numb the brain, hypnotizing and turning the mind to mush. The right half of the brain, which handles passive responses, is manipulated while the left hemisphere, which performs thought and analysis, remains unaffected, researchers say.

This is vividly demonstrated by hooking a viewer to an EEG, which measures brain waves. After a minute or so of watching the tube, the normal "Beta" waves that indicate alertness and focused attention disappear. Instead, "Alpha" waves take over, indicating a state of stupor. In short, the viewer, as most who have watched TV know, becomes "spaced out." This happens, researchers unanimously agree, no matter what program is being watched. That is one reason we tend to react to real deaths on the news the way we react to deaths on *Starsky and Hutch*—hardly at all. Drs. Erik Peper and Thomas Mulholland are among the hundreds who have studied the way viewing affects the brain. Concluded Peper: "The horror of television is that the information goes in, but we don't react to it."

This would not be as bad if, like other narcotics, the effects of TV viewing wore off after use. But scientists have discovered what is obvious from everyday observations: Those who watch TV tend to have trancelike lapses at all times. They have trouble analyzing events, and suffer from shorter attention spans. At times, they languish in passive mental states. At other times, perhaps because their minds have been bombarded with undigested images and their bodies have remained unnaturally immobile for long periods, they tend to be hyperactive.

These effects are particularly pronounced, and especially dangerous, in young children. Even though they may learn from *Sesame Street* what

Monologues

the letter *A* looks like, their cognitive skills are retarded. One reason is that their eye movements have been suppressed from staring at the tube. Another is that they see images but do not use their hands or other senses. Children learn by doing simple things—like putting pegs into holes, playing with clay, splashing cups and boats in a tub—activities they miss by watching TV. Kindergarten teachers report there is a decline in hand-eye coordination as well as the well-documented slump in reading and aptitude scores. As Kate Moody writes in *Growing Up on TV*: "Without motor commitment, learning can be drastically reduced."

The content of TV, like the medium itself, can be desensitizing, particularly in regard to violence. By the time an average child is fourteen, he or she will have witnessed 14,000 TV murders. There are eight major, noncomic acts of violence in an hour of prime-time TV. As social critic Erma Bombeck once wrote to TV network executives: "During a single evening I saw 12 people shot, two tortured, one dumped into a swimming pool, two cars explode, a rape, and a man who crawled two blocks with a knife in his stomach. Do you know something? I didn't feel anger or shock or horror or excitement or repugnance. The truth is I didn't feel. Through repeated assaults of one violent act after another, you have taken from me something I valued—the instinct to feel."

In the 1972 surgeon general's report *Television and Social Behavior*, each of the dozen experts involved found a relationship between TV violence and aggressive behavior. The summary of the fifty lab studies showed that viewing TV violence makes children more willing to harm others. Ten years later, the National Institute of Mental Health reviewed new studies on the issue. The conclusion: "Television violence is as strongly correlated with aggressive behavior as any other behavioral variant that has been measured." After the TV broadcast of a scene of Russian roulette recently, twenty-nine people shot themselves imitating the act. Other televised crimes copied by younger viewers include giving a teacher poisoned candy, putting ground glass in the family stew, and raping a young girl with a broomstick handle. A study of a hundred juvenile offenders found that twenty-two admitted copying criminal techniques from TV. Excessive TV viewing has even been tried as a legal defense for violent acts.

In subtle ways, the view of the world TV implants in our psyche is grossly distorted. Arguments tend to end with fists flying, scores are settled with guns. The consumption of junk foods and battery-operated toys is glamorized in the more than one thousand commercials the average viewer sees in a week. The warped values that suffuse the problem-plagued, designer-decorated living rooms of both soap opera and sitcom families become more familiar than our own. We begin to see normality as a cross between *Laverne & Shirley* and *Dallas*. Victims of the TV age are alienated from their own personal values and social surroundings and shut off from active involvement in the real world by the hypnotic pull of the airwaves. Instead of participating in life, they passively view a distortion of it.

In sum, television is neither a source of inspiration, as Edward R. Murrow hoped, nor merely wires and lights in a box, as he feared. It has become something even worse. By its very nature, and through the programs it presents, it is a source of mental illness. As the National Institute of Mental Health concluded: "Television can no longer be considered as a casual part of daily life, as an electronic toy. Research findings have long since destroyed the illusion that television is merely innocuous entertainment." It is time that we turned on to life by tuning out the tube.

Tuning In

According to data from the A. C. Nielsen Co. compiled by *U.S. News & World Report* (August 2, 1982), TV use in the United States has reached the following levels:

AVERAGE DAILY HOUSEHOLD VIEWING	
1951	4 hours, 35 minutes
1961	5 hours, 9 minutes
1971	6 hours, 1 minute
1981	6 hours, 44 minutes

WEEKLY VIEWING HABITS	
Women 55 and over	36 hours, 33 minutes
Men 55 and over	33 hours, 15 minutes
Women 18 to 55	31 hours, 49 minutes
Men 18 to 55	28 hours, 3 minutes
Teenagers	22 hours, 59 minutes
Children 2 to 11	25 hours, 10 minutes

VIII

How Good Is the Evidence:
Are the Samples Representative
and the Measurements Valid?

Thus far, you have been working at taking the raw materials a writer gives you and assembling them into a meaningful overall structure. You have learned ways to filter out the irrelevant parts and ways to discover the "invisible glue" that holds the relevant parts together—that is, the assumptions. You have learned to do this by asking critical questions.

Let's briefly review these questions.

1. What are the issue and the conclusion?
2. What are the reasons?
3. What words or phrases are ambiguous?
4. What are the value conflicts and assumptions?
5. What are the definitional and descriptive assumptions?

Most of the remaining chapters of the book will focus on how well the structure holds up after being assembled. Your major question now is, How acceptable is the conclusion? You are now ready to **evaluate**. *Remember:* The objective of critical reading is to judge the acceptability or worth of the different conclusions that can be reached concerning an issue. Making these judgments will prepare you for forming a rational personal opinion—the ultimate benefit of asking the right questions.

You begin the evaluative process by raising issues of *fact*, or *truth*. Virtually all arguments include factual claims—statements about what the world is like, was like, or will be like. The following are examples of factual claims:

Capital punishment acts as a deterrent to crime.

Marijuana causes brain damage.

Speed reading increases comprehension.

In order to evaluate, you need to decide whether or not to believe these claims. You should be asking, How true are such claims?

There are several paths to truth. One of the most powerful is the use of *empirical evidence*—evidence collected through human observation and experiment. The next three chapters focus on questions you should ask about empirical evidence so that you can decide to what degree the writer has provided appropriate evidence for his factual claims.

One of the most common methods for providing empirical evidence for a factual claim is to collect research data from a selected sample of people and then to infer a general principle from these specific findings. The major question you want to ask about this kind of reasoning is, Are the samples representative and the measurements valid?

⬦ *Critical Question:* **Are the samples representative and the measurements valid?**

Evidence as a Guide to Informed Opinion

All of us are constantly stating opinions, frequently in the form of generalizations. Generalizations are statements made about a large group of instances when only a smaller group of those instances have been studied. For example, when a conclusion is made about the quality of swimmers in California and only a *few* California swimmers have been observed, the conclusion is a generalization. Thus, the statement, "California swimmers are stronger than Oregon swimmers" is a generalization. You can encounter such generalizations daily, in statements such as

Jogging is good for your health.

College is a waste of time and money.

Saccharine causes cancer.

Politicians are crooked.

Brushing your teeth reduces cavities.

Decreasing taxes will stimulate the economy.

You encounter these generalizations when you talk to friends, visit your local mechanic, read *Reader's Digest* and *Time*, watch television commercials, read textbooks, and listen to lectures. How does one know when such opinions are "true"?

Determining the truth of an opinion is an extremely difficult task. In the first place, many of us feel so intensely about some of our value assumptions that we will hold tightly to particular opinions regardless of how much evidence those who disagree may present. For example, persons who strongly consider abortion immoral will resist considering evidence about the benefits of permitting legal abortions. For evidence to have any impact on us, we first have to give it a chance. Openness to evidence is one of the basic attitudes that you should try to develop. Otherwise, you will prematurely cease to learn.

A second problem in determining the worth of an opinion is that some questions or controversies are by their very nature especially difficult to answer. For instance, some issues require *instant* action such that no satisfactory evidence can be gathered and organized. If your mother claims that she has severe pain in her chest, you decide immediately to take her to the hospital. You do not pause to question the legitimacy of the pain or to survey her friends to see whether she complains of pain frequently as a means of getting attention. In such a situation, evidence is not pertinent as the basis for your decision.

Many types of questions can be answered with the aid of evidence. But some questions, particularly those which focus on human behavior, can be answered only tentatively even with the best of evidence. Human behavior is so complex and varied that evidence will only provide us with statements about what may *probably* happen. No amount of evidence, for example, would enable us to say with absolute confidence that a particular person would be a good spouse. What evidence does provide for such questions is a presumption or a shifting of the burden of proof. If the evidence is better for opinion A, then I will presume that it is a superior opinion until those who disagree can prove that A is incorrect. For example, the scientific evidence thus far suggests that it is *highly probable* that smoking causes lung cancer. Thus I will choose not to smoke until I have reason to believe that smoking does not cause cancer.

You will no doubt recognize that other types of questions can be answered precisely with the aid of evidence. Examples of such questions are the following:

Do most freshmen on our campus claim that they have cheated?

Did former Presidents give newly elected Presidents foreign policy briefings during the 1970s and 1980s?

Has the number of jails in our country increased during the last decade?

These questions can be answered correctly only after evidence has been gathered.

The value of an opinion, as you can now see, is partially dependent on the type of question it is attempting to answer. Although *truth* has many definitions, we will define it in a particular way in this chapter. A statement is true when it is in accordance with the facts. A fact is an event, state of existence, or relationship for which reliable evidence can be found. Thus, the key to determining whether or not a statement is true is in finding the evidence for the statement. What kind of evidence should you require? Let's take a look at the following factual claim:

> An individual's handwriting is a useful guide to her personality.

How do you know whether or not to believe this generalization? Through your own experience? Not likely, since you probably have little or no relevant experience. Through the reports of a graphologist—that is, someone who interprets handwriting? Isn't he likely to be biased, since he makes his living reading handwriting? By asking an expert psychologist? How do you know if she has subjected the question to careful analysis? What evidence does she have? The preferable course is to examine the results of a research study in which many careful observations have been recorded by trained observers—in this case, a study in which the personality descriptions made by graphologists are compared with other indicators of an individual's personality. This option gets us closest to objective evidence—the facts. A statement based on such evidence will be closer to the truth than will one based on personal experience, an uncritical appeal to authorities, or an appeal to biased observers.

Once a factual claim has been backed up by carefully collected evidence, it no longer is simply an opinion; it is an *informed opinion*, and the claim has a greater probability of being true. Can you now clearly see that some opinions are better than others? Someone who argues that any opinion is always as good as any other is wrong! Such an argument would be true only if all opinions were equally worthless, with no evidence provided to support any of them. An individual has a right to his own opinion in the same way that an individual has a right to be ignorant. This view is aptly reflected in the following quote by Bernard Baruch: "Every man has a right to his opinion, but no man has a right to be wrong in the facts."

Dangers of Personal Experience as a Guide to the Facts

There is a crucial difference between personal experience and experience under controlled observation. There are a number of agreed-upon standards for judging whether something has been established as a fact. The average person who cites "personal experience" has not applied these standards and thus is subject to many practical errors. You can see some of these practical errors by reflecting on how you might answer the following question: Does watching too much violence on television increase the tendency to commit a violent act? Let's take a look at some common errors.

1. *Paying attention only to experience that favors a belief (and ignoring instances that contradict the belief).* You can always find a number of violent people who watch a lot of television. But are you keeping track of the nonviolent people? Perhaps they also watch television often.

2. *Generalizing from only a few experiences.* Maybe you are familiar with a couple of cases in which people committed crimes similar to those committed in a television show. Perhaps they would have committed these crimes anyway.

3. *Failing to "keep track" of events, to count, to control.* How good is your memory? Not as good as careful records!

4. *Oversimplifying.* We sometimes fail to consider that there are other characteristics in addition to those in which we are interested that might be affecting the behaviors under observation. You recall an incident in which a juvenile vandalized a school, just after watching a juvenile gang film on television. But maybe that youth was imitating his violent parents.

Remember: Beware of the individual who says, "My experience proves . . ." or "I can disprove all that because of an experience I had. . . ." The critical reader is always skeptical of experiences, subjects them to critical analysis, and determines whether they have been adequately confirmed by appropriate observational methods.

Look closely at the following two arguments. You should now be able to see that Argument B is better because it provides objective evidence. It does not rely merely on personal experience.

Argument A

Certain Bay Area physicians, nurses, social workers, psychologists, and psychiatrists find that graphoanalysis provides a time-saving approach to understanding their clients and patients. In all these instances, graphoanalysts (handwriting analysts) and those who have been exposed to graphoanalytic assessment have found that this "soft science" is an accurate personality projection technique. . . . Practicing graphoanalysts know it works because they see the proof every day in their jobs.

Argument B

In a university experiment, graphologists completed a graphoanalysis (personality description based on handwriting) on 48 students. After the results were collected, each student was provided with two graphoanalysis reports. One was his own report, and one was randomly selected from the reports of the other 47 students. Each student was then asked to select the report that best described his own personality. More than half the students selected the wrong report. The researchers concluded that graphoanalysis has questionable validity.

The Scientific Method

Because the relationships among events in our world are so complex, and because humans are fallible in the way that they observe and theorize about these events, we have turned to the *scientific method* as an important guide to determining the facts. The scientific method attempts to avoid many of the built-in biases in our observations of the world and in our intuition and common sense.

What is special about the scientific method? Above all, it seeks information in the form of *verifiable data*—that is, data obtained under conditions such that other qualified people can make similar observations and obtain the same results. This *objective evidence* is the kind we are usually calling for when we ask, "Where is your evidence?"

A second major characteristic of scientific method is *control*—that is, minimizing extraneous factors that might affect the accuracy and interpretation of generalizations. Physical scientists frequently maximize control by studying problems in the laboratory. When researchers do experiments, they attempt to minimize extraneous factors. Unfortunately, control is usually more difficult in the social world than in the physical world; thus it is very difficult to successfully apply the scientific method to many questions about human behavior.

Precision in language is a third major component of the scientific method. Our concepts are often confusing, obscure, and ambiguous. Scientific method attempts to be precise and consistent in the use of language.

While there is much more to science than we can discuss here, we want you to keep in mind that the best evidence is usually that which is *verifiable by others*, *obtained under controlled conditions*, and *precisely communicated*.

Unfortunately, the fact that research has been applied to a problem does not necessarily mean that the scientific evidence is good evidence. Science is not infallible and cannot adequately address some questions.

While the best argument is usually the one that supports its factual claims by reference to relevant, objective, and up-to-date data from the best sources possible, much research evidence is flawed.

Probabilistic Generalizations

Most of us recognize that generalizations require some type of evidence to provide support for their accuracy. Therefore, you will often encounter evidence attached to a generalization. Let's examine a brief example.

> Despite their discontent, city dwellers have fewer mental health prob-lems than their rural counterparts. . . . The survey reported on 6,700 interviews with adults who lived in one of six community sizes, ranging from cities with populations of over 3,000,000 to rural towns of less than 2,500. The findings were based on symptoms the respondents themselves reported, such as difficulty in sleeping, and either expecting or having had a nervous breakdown. People living in cities of over 50,000 showed symptom scores that were almost 20 percent lower than those of people in communities of less than 50,000.

Let's isolate the structure of this argument.

CONCLUSION: *City dwellers have fewer mental health problems than their rural counterparts.*

REASON: *A survey shows that people living in cities of over 50,000 showed symptom scores that were almost 20 percent lower than those of people in communities of less than 50,000.*

First, note that the conclusion is a generalization. The conclusion is about city and rural dwellers *in general*. It would have been impossible to study *all* city and rural dwellers. Consequently, a *sample* of 6,700 was stud-ied, and a generalization was formed on the basis of the sample.

Second, note that the evidence supporting the generalization is in the form of *statistics*—that is, facts of a numerical kind which have been assem-bled, classified, and tabulated so as to present significant information. Thus, the generalization is a *statistical generalization*. Third, note that the gener-alization that "city dwellers have fewer mental health problems than their rural counterparts" is a *probabilistic generalization*. Why? Because the gen-eralization is *not uniform*; it does not apply in all cases. In the example, we can say only that *on the average* a city dweller is *more likely* to have lower

symptom scores. We cannot say that *all* city dwellers will have lower symptom scores than *all* rural dwellers. Few generalizations dealing with the behavior of people will be in the form, "All A are B"; most will be probabilistic generalizations, such as, "Some A's are B," or "More A's than B's are C."

Since probabilistic generalizations are not uniform, what good are they? If they are not true in all cases, doesn't that mean that such generalizations are not true? No, not at all! Even though the generalization is probabilistic, it still may be true. Certainly it may be true that on the average urban dwellers have fewer symptoms than rural dwellers. What is not true is that every city dweller will be better off. It is useful to know that on the average they differ, since that recognition may lead to very different conclusions about the impact of city living. Thus, note that with probabilistic generalizations, *exceptions do not disprove the generalizations*; in fact, exceptions are expected. When someone states a probabilistic generalization, she does not have to assume that her assertion is true for everybody in order for the generalization to be correct.

Elements of Statistical Generalizations

Every statistical argument will have

1. *A target population*—the group of individuals or events one wants to generalize about. In the above case, the target population is city and rural dwellers.
2. *A sample*—a subgroup of the target population. We cannot observe everyone we want to generalize about, so we observe *some* members of the group—a sample. In this case, the sample consisted of 6,700 adults living in one of six community sizes.
3. *The characteristic of interest*—that aspect of the target population that we want to generalize about. In this case, the characteristic of interest was mental health problems.

Representativeness of the Sample

It should now be clear that the nature of the sample is crucial. When is a sample adequate to permit leaping to a general conclusion? When it is *representative* of the target population. For example, if you wanted to generalize about college students in the United States, you would not want to sample only students from a midwestern college, because that sample would not be representative of the target population. When is a sample representative? When it has had sufficient *size*, *breadth*, and *randomness*.

The size of a sample is crucial. The more cases in a sample, the better. There is no absolute guide to the number needed, but the smaller the number, the less faith we can have in the generalization. Clearly, a sample of one, or just a few, is not enough. Such a sample will be *biased*. You would certainly not be satisfied if the Gallup poll sampled only five people, since these five people might differ markedly from most of the population—that is, they might be nonrepresentative. However, with a sample of 5,000 people, the opinions will become more representative. Or how about the type of commercial that says, "Four out of five doctors recommend Painstop Aspirin?" You would be quite skeptical if only five doctors had been questioned, we hope. **Examine the size of the sample!**

In addition to the need for large size, a *broad-spectrum* sample is preferred to a *narrow band*. When is a sample sufficiently broad? Only when one samples across all important characteristics of the target population. For example, when one samples only male undergraduates at a midwestern university as to their attitudes toward alcohol consumption, one can generalize only about male undergraduates in midwestern universities. However, if one samples both male and female undergraduates from universities and colleges in all sections of the United States and from all class levels (freshmen, sophomores, juniors, and seniors) one can then generalize about American undergraduates. It is also important to sample *proportionately*. If 60 percent of undergraduates are female, it is optimal for 60 percent of the sample to be female. **Examine the breadth of the sample!** Ask how well the sample characteristics mirror those of the population.

You have probably heard the phrase *random sampling* many times. Both the Gallup poll and the Nielsen ratings sample randomly. What makes a sample *random?* A sample is random when the individuals or events sampled are selected by a chance process, which serves to prevent bias. Each member from the group to be sampled should have the same opportunity to be selected. For example, if one is interested in how freshmen view their first quarter in school, one does not simply select the first 15 freshmen she encounters at the Student Union. Why? Students who go to the Union may be quite different in attitudes from those who are at the library, or from those who are studying at a fraternity or sorority. Such a sample will be biased, and will not mirror the freshman population. One means of overcoming the bias would be to take names at random from the student telephone directory, perhaps by calling every fifteenth person in the directory. **Examine the randomness of the sample!** Were subjects or events selected on a random or chance basis, or were they selected in some systematically biased fashion?

Now that you are aware of the major questions you should ask about the sample, let's determine the appropriateness of the sample in a brief generalization argument.

Is the kid who sleeps with a toy gun destined to become the local bully? Not at all, maintain University of Nebraska psychologists Joseph C. LaVoie and Gerald Adams. To find out how much kids really know about firearms, the investigators interviewed 73 middle-class children (37 boys and 36 girls) ranging in age from five to ten. The children were then tested for verbal and physical aggression. It was found that gunplay and aggression did not go together. Kids who played with guns and those who did not scored the same number of both physical and verbal aggression points.[1]

The structure of this argument is as follows:

CONCLUSION: *Playing with guns does not lead to physical aggression.*

REASON: *When tested for verbal and physical aggression, kids who played with guns and those who didn't had the same number of physical and verbal aggression points.*

Let's examine the size, breadth, and randomness of the sample. Seventy-three children were tested; thus, we can have some confidence that the results are relatively stable. How about the breadth? The sample covers both boys and girls, and a fairly wide age range; thus, results can legitimately be generalized across both sexes and the age range from five to ten. But the sample may have been drawn only from families in a university community. Results might have been different if the researchers had selected children who had not been affected strongly by the more peaceful values of a university community. Can you think of other characteristics that should have been considered? How about intelligence levels? Maybe children with low intelligence differ from children with high intelligence in how they are affected by playing with guns.

How about randomness? We cannot determine this from the above description. Optimally, these 73 children should have been randomly selected from a larger population of children. Were these the first 73 children to volunteer for the project? If so, what factors might have led to their volunteering? Perhaps they came from families who had a great deal of confidence in their children's social competence. If so, the sample is biased. Be sure to think about *why* the sample might be biased before you go on to the next section.

That sample selection has a major impact on findings is aptly illustrated by popular polls. On August 15, 1984, five different polls reported

[1]"Toy Guns and Aggression," *Human Behavior* (April 1975), 73.

the percentage of respondents who said they preferred President Reagan or Walter Mondale. The results were as follows:

Poll	Findings
New York Times/CBS News	Reagan 52%, Mondale 34%
NBC News	Reagan 60%, Mondale 34%
ABC News	Reagan 44%, Mondale 43%
Louis Harris & Associates	Reagan 51%, Mondale 46%
Gallup Poll	Reagan 52%, Mondale 42%

Let's summarize what you should ask when you encounter a leap from evidence about a sample to a generalization about a larger population. First, ask the question, How representative is the sample? Then your answer will be determined by the size, breadth, and randomness of the sample. *Remember*: You should generalize only to a population that is mirrored by the sample, and it is your job to determine which important characteristics should be mirrored.

Hasty Generalizations

When a generalization is stated on the basis of a sample that is too small or biased to warrant the generalization, the *hasty generalization* fallacy is committed, meaning that one has jumped to the conclusion too quickly. A frequent kind of hasty generalization is to jump to a conclusion concerning "all" on the basis of just a few examples. For example, if someone sees a few poor women drivers, then asserts that all women are poor drivers, he is committing the fallacy of hasty generalization.

Note that while it is important that hasty generalizations be avoided, we should not avoid making sound generalizations—that is, assertions that are compatible with the evidence. If statistics from a dozen studies with appropriate size, breadth, and randomness tell us that 25 percent of the people who take a certain drug to cure cancer go blind, we should seriously consider banning the drug—even though not *all* people taking the drug will go blind, and 25 percent may not be the *exact* probability. We act because we have some degree of confidence that 25 percent approximates the true figure.

Let's take a look at a recent survey on male sexuality to see how inadequate sampling can lead to hasty generalizations. *The Hite Report on Male Sexuality* presents generalizations based on questionnaires; but of the

119,000 questionnaires distributed, only 7,239 were returned. Nearly half of these replies came from men who had read Hite's earlier books, who answered versions of the questionnaire reprinted in magazines like *Penthouse*, or who knew about Hite's work from television and radio appearances. Could this sample be representative? How much faith would you put in generalizations based on this survey? Not much, we hope.

Because the way people respond to surveys is affected by many unknown factors, such as the need to please or the interpretation of the question, should we *ever* treat survey evidence as good evidence? There are heated debates about this issue, but our answer is yes, as long as we are careful. For example, we think auto-industry survey findings that only 15 percent of the population wears seat belts should be considered in making judgments about inserting air bags in cars. We give less credibility, however, to magazine surveys that tell us that most Americans are happily married. Some findings are simply more compelling than others. You will have to make subjective judgments based on the available evidence.

Validity of the Measurements

After you have asked about the representativeness of the sample, you must then ask, How well has the characteristic of interest been measured? Evidence supporting generalizations usually consists of measurements of individuals or events in the sample. You should ask certain questions about such measurements before accepting them. To illustrate, let's examine the characteristic of interest in the example in the last section with attention to the quality of its measurement. First, let's restate the conclusion: Playing with guns does not lead to *physical aggression*.

We have italicized the significant characteristic. How did the researchers measure physical aggression? "Tests" were used. The question you should ask is, Do these tests validly measure physical aggression? You cannot assume that something measures a characteristic just because it claims to. Because of a variety of influences, many tests are not valid; they do not measure what they claim to measure. Thus, it is the obligation of the person using the measurement device to provide evidence for its validity. Perhaps physical aggression was measured in these studies by teachers' reports of the child's activity in a structured situation. It is possible that such reports do not reflect the child's aggressive behavior in less structured situations. You should always ask the question, What is the evidence that the measurement is a valid measurement of the characteristic? If there is no evidence, this greatly weakens the quality of the generalization.

When the characteristic of interest is measured, ask, Are the meaurements valid? What evidence is there that they measure what they are supposed to measure?

Biased Surveys

One of the measuring devices you will encounter most frequently is the *survey*. Think how often you hear the phrase "according to recent polls." Surveys are usually used to measure people's attitudes and beliefs. Conclusions based on surveys require the assumption that verbal reports (for example, "I definitely believe that busing is a good thing") accurately reflect true attitudes (for example, "I am willing to let my kid be bused"). *This is always a questionable assumption.* Because of this problem, survey evidence must always be treated with caution. For example, many individuals try to give answers that they think they ought to give rather than answers that reflect their true beliefs.

In addition, surveys can contain *built-in biases* which make them even more suspect. Biased wording of questions is a common problem. Let's examine a conclusion based on a recent poll and then look at the survey question.

A U.S. Congressman sent a questionnaire to his constituents and received the following results: 92 percent were against government-supported child care centers.

Now let's look closely at the survey question: Do you believe the federal government should provide child care centers to assist parents in rearing their children? Look carefully at this question. Do you see the built-in bias? The "leading" words are "to assist parents in rearing their children." Wouldn't the responses have been quite different if the question had read, Do you believe the federal government should provide child care centers to assist parents who are unable to find alternative child care while they are working? Thus, the measurement obtained here is not a valid indicator of attitudes concerning child care centers.

Survey data must always be examined for possible bias. Look carefully at the wording of the questions! Here is another example. We have italicized the word that evidences the bias.

QUESTION: Do you think that a person with a homosexual *disorder* should be permitted to teach your innocent children?

CONCLUSION: Seventy-five percent of the people do not want homosexuals to teach their children.

Using Generalizations in Your Writing

When you write essays, you will often want to make claims about groups of people. You may want to state their preferences or summarize their behavior. You will need to state a generalization.

What kind of evidence should you include? The answer to this question is dependent on the kind of issue about which you are writing. The first section in this chapter is the place to start. First, you know that evidence is desirable. Then, you learned that different amounts and qualities of evidence are required in different instances. Finally, you should use the standards for evaluating generalizations as a checklist to guide your use of evidence.

Since you will not usually be able to gather systematic evidence on your own, you should be cautious about the evidence you borrow from others. Check the quality of the sample and the extent to which the measurement is consistent with what it claims to be representing. Share with your readers the care you used in selecting the evidence. If you demonstrate that you have been highly selective in citing evidence, your writing will be more persuasive.

Summary

In this chapter, we have focused on the evaluation of generalizations. We have stressed that generalizations require reliable evidence before you can accept their truth. Thus, where appropriate, the first question to ask about a generalization is, Where is the evidence? We have provided you with some ways of determining whether statistical evidence for a generalization is *good evidence*. Let's review some of the ways to ascertain whether a writer is generalizing inappropriately.

1. First, determine whether there is *any* objective evidence.
2. If there is objective evidence, find out how representative the sample is. Check on its size, breadth, and randomness. If it fails on any of these dimensions, the sample will be biased, and you will have identified a hasty generalization.
3. Determine whether the writer or speaker is measuring what he claims to be measuring. Carefully compare the kind of measurement with the characteristic that is being generalized about.

Practice Exercises

In the three practice passages, evaluate the generalizations.

⸎   *Critical Question:*   **Are the samples representative and the measurements valid?**

Passage 1

A survey carried out by the National Science Foundation (NSF) shows there are marked differences in marital status between male and female psychologists, which document the incompatibility of marriage and a career for a good proportion of female psychologists. While 8 percent of male psychologists never marry, 22 percent of the women never marry. Five percent of the men are separated or divorced, while 13 percent of the women are. Seventy-five percent of the men in the general U.S. population are married, compared with 68 percent of the women.

Passage 2

What one learns in school is seldom of use on the job. For example, the Carnegie Commission queried all the employees with degrees in engineering or science in two large firms. Only one in five said the work they were doing bore a "very close relationship" to their college studies, while almost a third said "very little relationship at all." An overwhelming majority could think of many people who were doing the same work they were doing but had majored in different fields.

Passage 3

To what extent are adopted children more vulnerable to emotional and academic problems than their nonadopted peers? To answer this question, psychological and academic adjustments were evaluated in a sample of 130 adopted and 130 nonadopted children ranging in age from 6 through 11 years. Adjustment measures included maternal ratings on Achenbach's Child Behavior Profile and teacher ratings on the Hahneman Elementary School Behavior Rating Scale. Adoptive families were recruited from the New Jersey, Eastern Pennsylvania, and New York City areas through adoption support groups, adoption agencies, newspaper advertisements, and word of mouth. Nonadoptive families were recruited from five central and northern New Jersey school systems and through newspaper advertisements. Results indicated that adopted children were rated higher in psychological and school-related behavior problems and lower in social competence and school achievement than were nonadopted children. Although the results support the position that the risk of developing emotional and school-related problems is greater for adopted children, caution is urged against overinterpreting the data, because the majority of adopted children appear well adjusted.[2]

[2]Adapted from D. M. Brodzinski, D. E. Scheuhter, A. M. Braff, and L. M. Singer, "Psychological and Academic Adjustment in Adopted Children," *Journal of Consulting and Clinical Psychology* 52 (1984), 582–590.

––––––––––––––––––––––––––––––––   **SAMPLE RESPONSES**   ––––––––––––––––––––––––––––––––

Passage 1

First, let's assemble the structure of this argument.

CONCLUSION: *Marriage and a career are especially incompatible for a good proportion of female psychologists.*

REASONS: *1. There are marked differences in marital status between male and female psychologists. (a) A survey shows that while 8 percent of male psychologists never marry, 22 percent of the women never marry. Five percent of the men are separated or divorced, while 13 percent of the women are. Seventy-five percent of the men in the general U.S. population are married, compared with 68 percent of the women.*

The reason is a generalization supporting the conclusion. The evidence (a) is provided to support the reason. How strong is this evidence? First, we ask, *Is the sample representative of the population we are generalizing about?* In the conclusion, the relevant populations are male and female psychologists. From the data provided, we cannot tell the size, breadth, and randomness of the samples; thus, the samples could be biased. For example, maybe only a few female psychologists were willing to complete the survey data, whereas the majority of men completed it. However, the survey was completed by the National Science Foundation (NSF), which is relatively sophisticated about data collection. Thus, our best guess is that the sample is representative.

Next, we ask, *How valid are the measures?* In this case, the survey asks the respondents to indicate whether or not they are married. This is a very direct measure of the characteristic of interest in the generalization—the tendency to be in and to remain in a marriage relationship. The major assumption made is that males and females will be equally honest in reporting whether or not they are married.

Passage 2

CONCLUSION: *What one learns in school is seldom of use on the job.*

REASON: *When the Carnegie Commission queried all the employees with degrees in engineering or science in two large firms, only one in five said the work they were doing bore a "very close relationship" to their college studies. Also, an overwhelming majority could think of many people who were doing the same work but had majors in different fields.*

First, we note that the population being generalized about is college-educated people. Serious questions about sample representativeness can be raised. Only two kinds of degrees and two kinds of firms were utilized in the questioning process. It would have been much better to sample many firms and many different majors in order to obtain a representative sample of people who went to college. We can also question the validity of the measurement. Do verbal reports that a job does not bear a close relationship to college studies accurately indicate the usefulness of college education? One would question the ability of an individual to make such a judgment. Second, does the fact that one does not make specific use of one's major on the job suggest college education is useless? Not necessarily! Skills learned in college may be useful in many different jobs.

Thus, while the generalization in this passage is accompanied by some evidence, one can seriously question whether the samples were representative and whether the measures were valid.

Passage 3

CONCLUSION: *The risk of developing emotional and school-related problems is greater for adopted children.*

REASON: *Adopted children are rated higher in psychological and school-related behavior problems and lower in social competence and school achievement than are nonadopted children.*

This is a very common research design in the social sciences. The populations being generalized about are adopted and nonadopted children. The sample size is quite large. But, the information does not enable us to determine the breadth of the sample. Though multiple states were sampled, to what extent were the family sizes, family incomes, and ages of parents typical of adoptive families? Perhaps the most important sampling problem was the lack of a random sample. Given the recruiting procedures, were there selective factors that led certain kinds of parents to volunteer for the study, and were these selective procedures different for adoptive and nonadoptive families? Perhaps, for example, adoptive families are generally more willing to volunteer even if their children are experiencing problems. If such selective factors were operating, then the sample is biased.

How valid are the rating measurements? Can parent and teacher ratings be trusted to reflect emotional adjustment accurately? How ambiguous were the rating terms? How objective are parents and teachers in making their ratings? Does knowing that the child is adopted affect how one rates that child? We would want to know more about the validity of these scales before we could have much confidence in the conclusion.

Passage 4 (Self-Examination)

A recent study[3] shows evidence that modern boxers suffer brain damage from their sport. The researchers contacted by telephone 23 former boxers who (1) were aged 25 to 60 years, (2) were currently residing in the New York area, (3) had not retired from boxing for medical, neurological, or psychiatric reasons, (4) were retired from boxing for at least 1 year before the study, (5) had no known history of neurological, psychiatric, or serious medical illness, and (6) had no known history of drug or alcohol abuse. Fifteen former boxers and three active Golden Gloves fighters contacted the researchers and volunteered to participate. Thus, a total of 18 boxers participated in the study. The group included two former professional champions, three highly ranked professional contenders, and four other amateur champions; only one former fighter was primarily a "slugger"; all others were considered to be scientific, artful fighters who practiced self-defense.

Each boxer underwent neurological examinations, a computerized tomographic scan of the brain (a measure of brain atrophy), an electroencephalogram (EEG), and neuropsychological testing. The researchers found evidence of brain damage on at least two of the measures in 13 of the 15 professional boxers, and evidence of subtle brain damage in the three amateur boxers. The authors concluded that brain damage is a frequent result of a career in professional boxing.

Reasons
conclusion
How valid are the measures,
and wheather the sample is adequate.

The researchers contacted by phone 23 ✓
aged 25 to 60.
were retired from boxing at least 1 y,
Fflee.

[3]Adapted from I. R. Casson, O. Siegel, R. Sham, E. A. Campbell, M. Tarlau, and A. Di-Domenico, "Brain Damage in Modern Boxers," *Journal of the American Medical Association* 251 (May 25, 1984), 2663–2667.

IX

How Good Is the Evidence:
Are There Flaws
in the Statistical Reasoning?

In the previous chapter, our primary focus was on helping you to determine when sampling procedures and measurements are adequate to support generalizations. In this chapter, we continue to focus on evidence by highlighting some of the more common ways by which people play tricks with statistics. Statistics can easily deceive. To avoid being deceived, always ask yourself, What evidence would be most helpful in reaching this conclusion? Then look at the evidence presented. If the two do not match, you have probably located a statistical error. We recognize, however, that it is frequently difficult to know just what evidence should be provided. To help you to get a better idea of what types of evidence are flawed, this chapter illustrates a number of different ways to "lie" with statistics.

◊   Critical Question: ***Are there flaws in the statistical reasoning?***

Evidence from Authority: Testimony

You encounter appeals to many forms of authority on a daily basis.

> Movie reviewers: "One of the ten best movies of the year."—Valerie Viewer, *Toledo Gazette.*
> Organizations: "The American Medical Association supports this position."
> Athletes: "Touchdown Beer is a real competitor."—Bill Battle, quarterback.
> Researchers: "Studies show . . ."
> Relatives: "My grandfather says . . ."
> Religion: "The Koran says . . ."
> Magazines: "According to *Newsweek* . . ."

You can easily add to our list. It should be obvious that some appeals to authority should be taken much more seriously as evidence than others. Why? Because some authorities are much more careful in giving an opinion than others. For example, *Newsweek* and *Time* are much more likely to carefully evaluate the available evidence prior to stating an opinion than is the *National Enquirer*. Athletes are less likely to have evaluated a political candidate than are editorial writers for major newspapers.

What should you do when you encounter appeals to authority? Be wary! Ask yourself questions concerning the expertise of the authority. Does the authority have special access to objective evidence? Is the authority respected by others in its field? Does it have experience in the field it is discussing? Has it had a history of being reliable? Is it likely to be objective in its judgment? Is it up to date?

Striking Examples

Writers frequently support their points by presenting what seem to be compelling examples, rather than by citing carefully collected research evidence. Watch out when this happens! You are likely to be fooled. Some examples can be found that will appear to support almost any generalization that a writer wishes to make. *Examples by themselves do not prove a point!* Let's see why. A few sample arguments in which examples are used to help prove a point follow.

> The effect of aging on people's mental processes has been overrated. Older people are able to accomplish a lot more than most people think they can. Look at what Winston Churchill accomplished after the age of 60. We should not make people retire until they are ready.

It is true that Winston Churchill accomplished a lot after the age of 60. But ask yourself, Is it possible for the example to be true, yet the conclusion not be true? The answer is yes. Perhaps Winston Churchill is not *typical* of older people. Perhaps there are many examples of older people's mental processes deteriorating rapidly after 65. Perhaps there were special circumstances that facilitated the accomplishments of Churchill.

So you see why the example does not *prove* the point? It is merely *consistent with* the conclusion. Let's look at another example.

> I know a man who smoked three packs of cigarettes a day and lived to be 89.

But how about all those men who smoked three packs a day and died before age 60?

Vivid case studies are striking examples that you must be especially wary of. Dramatic case studies are very concrete and easy to visualize, but such studies frequently blind us to relevant research evidence. For example, a detailed description of an obese welfare mother who has been irresponsible, has lived on welfare for 10 years, has lived with multiple husbands, and has had children by each of them may lead you to ignore the more relevant statistical data that only 10 percent of recipients remain on welfare rolls for 4 years or longer. Or, as another example, consider the power that viewing the aftermath of a gory car accident may have in influencing your beliefs about the importance of seat belts, as opposed to statistical data put out by the Surgeon General's office.

Be wary of examples as proof. Though examples will be *consistent* with the conclusion, do not let that consistency fool you. Always ask yourself, Is the example *typical*? Are there powerful counterexamples? Are there other explanations for the example?

Misleading Percentages

There has been a 50 percent increase in sales of widgets, as compared to only a 25 percent increase for our competitors.

Our steel product is 30 percent stronger than ever before.

Both these examples use percentages, and the numbers are quite impressive. But important information has been omitted. Do you see what it is? The *absolute numbers* on which the percentages are based are not given. Maybe sales of widgets increased from 40 units to 60 units (that's 50 percent), while competitors' sales increased from 10,000 to 12,500 units (that's only 25 percent). Which increase seems more impressive now? Look at the second example again. Don't we need to know how strong the product was before it was strengthened?

When you encounter percentages, always ask yourself, What numbers are the percentages based upon? Be especially cautious when a writer *compares* percentages.

It is important to know not only the absolute numbers on which the percentages are based, but also the absolute amount referred to by the percentages. For example, a small percentage does not necessarily mean an insignificant number. The following examples illustrate.

Air bags are safe; they would malfunction in only 0.1 percent of our cars.

But if there are more than 150 million cars on the road, that's 150,000 total malfunctions. What if the malfunctions lead to serious accidents?

Our proposed relaxing of the emission standards will result in a reduction of atmospheric ozone levels of only 2 percent by the late 1990s.

Might not 2 percent be significant? Maybe that 2 percent will be an amount large enough to prevent serious changes in our climate.

When you encounter percentages, ask yourself, Are there any absolute amounts I need to know before evaluating the evidence?

Impressively Large Numbers

(1) Seven hundred eighty-five psychiatrists support the insanity defense.

(2) More than 10,500 people have bought Panthers this year, making it our biggest year ever.

These numbers are meant to impress. But what important information is missing? In (1), don't we need to know how many psychiatrists were sent questionnaires, how many responded, and how qualified they were? In (2), wouldn't a percentage increase have been more meaningful? Maybe the increase was from 10,400 to 10,500, while other car sales were increasing at a much larger rate.

Lee Iacocca, president of Chrysler, put impressively large numbers into a different context to support his attempt to obtain a $1.2 billion loan guarantee from the federal government. He pointed out to a congressional committee that $409 billion of loan guarantees had already been granted by the government. The $1.2 billion was less impressive in this context than it ordinarily would have been.

Be wary of absolute numbers. Look for important omitted information.

Ambiguous Averages

Examine the following statements.

(1) Americans are better off than ever; the average salary of an American worker is now $23,400.

(2) The average pollution of air by factories is now well below the dangerous level.

Both examples use the word *average*. But there are three different ways to determine an average, and in most cases each will give you a different average. What are the three ways? One is to add up all the values and divide this total by the number of values used. The result is the *mean*.

A second way is to list all the values from highest to lowest, then find the one in the middle. This middle value is the *median*. Half of the values will be above the median; half will be below it. A third way is to list all the values and then count each different value or range of values. The value that appears most frequently is called the *mode*, the third kind of average.

It makes a big difference whether a writer is talking about the mean, median, or mode. Think about the salary distribution in the United States. Some individuals are paid extremely high salaries, such as $800,000 per year. Such high salaries will increase the mean dramatically. They will have little effect, however, on either the median or the mode. Thus, if one wishes to make the average salary seem high, the mean is probably the best average to present. You should now be able to see how important it is to know which average is used when people talk about salaries or income.

Now, let's look carefully at example (2). If the average presented is either the mode or the median, we may be tricked into a false sense of security. For example, what if only a few factories pollute highly, but the amount they pollute is far above the dangerous level—so far above that the air as a whole is still being dangerously polluted. In such a case, the mode and the median pollution values could be quite low, but the mean would be very high.

When you see "average" values, always ask, Does it matter whether it is the mean, the median, or the mode? To answer this, consider how the significance of the information might be changed by using the various meanings of *average*.

The Missing Range and Distribution

Not only is it important to determine whether an average is a mean, median, or mode, but it is often also important to determine the gap between the smallest and largest values—the *range*—and how frequently each of the values occurs—the *distribution*. For example, assume that you have to make the decision about whether to eat some fish caught in a nearby ocean. Would you be satisfied with information about the *average* mercury content in those fish? We wouldn't. We would want to know the *range* of mercury content—that is, the highest and lowest levels possible—as well as the *frequency* of the different levels. The average may be in the "safe" level; but if 10 percent of the fish contained levels of mercury well above the "safe" level, we suspect that you would rather eat something else for supper.

Let's consider another example in which knowing the range and distribution would be important.

America is not overcrowded. Nationally we have fewer than 60 people per square mile, a population density lower than that of most other countries.

First, we suspect that this population density figure represents the mean. While the mean density may be quite low, there obviously are areas in the United States—the Southwest, for example—with very low density figures. Thus, America may indeed be overcrowded in some areas, even though on the average it is not.

Thus, when an average is presented, ask yourself, Would it be important for me to know the range and distribution of values?

Concluding One Thing; Proving Another

The following example illustrates a common error in the use of statistics. Can you find it?

> A sorority dance was considered a huge success by its planners because only four people out of the 200 in attendance complained. "When only four people are discontented, and 196 are delighted," one of the planners was heard to say, "as far as I'm concerned, that's a successful dance."

Look first at what has actually been proven by the evidence: Most of the people attending the dance did not complain. The writer has no evidence that people attending were delighted. The appropriate evidence for such a conclusion is missing. The conclusion that people liked the dance would best be supported by evidence from a random sample of the people attending. One cannot assume that not complaining has the same meaning as being delighted.

Let's look at another example.

> A survey conducted at a certain college revealed that only a minority of girls were in favor of remaining virgins until the day they marry. The college newspaper wrote up the results under the headline "Most Coeds Favor Promiscuity."

The author has proved one thing but concluded another. The questionnaire concerned attitudes toward premarital virginity, not promiscuity. If the survey had asked, Do you favor promiscuity?, we suspect that it would have produced a very different conclusion from the one stated.

How do you catch such erroneous proofs? Ask yourself, What evidence is *needed* to prove the point?, and compare your answer with the evidence provided.

Summary

In this chapter, we have highlighted a number of ways in which you can catch people "lying" with statistics. The following is a list of all the ways we have discussed.

1. Be wary of *appeals to authority*. Examine the authority's expertise carefully.
2. Don't be fooled by *striking examples*. A single example is rarely good evidence.
3. When you encounter percentages, ask about the numbers on which the percentages are based, as well as the absolute amounts referred to by the percentages.
4. When you encounter *impressively large numbers*, determine what percentages would be useful to know before you interpret the statistics.
5. When an average is presented, determine whether it would be important to know if it is the mean, mode, or median.
6. When an average is presented, determine whether or not it would be important to know the range and distribution of the scores.
7. Form *your* conclusion from the evidence. If it doesn't match the writer's, something is probably wrong.

Practice Exercises

◊   *Critical Question:*   **Are there flaws in the statistical reasoning?**

For each of the three practice passages, identify inadequacies in the evidence supporting the generalization.

Passage 1

Americans in general are spoiled. Most of us tend to judge the times in relative terms—and we have had rich relatives.

Materially, no people on earth have ever been as well off. So, when most of us say "times are bad," we say it in a comfortable home, with a well-stocked electric refrigerator, television, and electric laundry equipment.

One in every 5 households in America in 1980 was affluent (had an income over $25,000). Twenty-five years ago, only 1 in 33 households was this comfortable. Our personal income, disposable income, and personal savings have all climbed continuously since 1950.

True, we still have a vast army of poor in the country. One in every 8 Americans is living below the poverty level—1 in every 4 aged 65 or over is poor. But twenty years ago, 1 in every 5 citizens was below the poverty line. In 7 years, more than 14 million of us have climbed out of the poverty hole.

Any country in which, while population increased 56 percent, home ownership increased 100 percent, car ownership 130 percent, and personal savings 696 percent, is a long way from hard times. That's what happened here between 1946 and 1980.

Passage 2

To justify so radical a departure from traditional forms of health care, proponents might claim that health services in America are so poor that greater governmental intrusion is imperative. Their argument makes little sense. Since 1970, infant mortality has dropped 30 percent, life expectancy has risen by a year, and nine of the ten leading causes of death have declined.

While the distribution of doctors is uneven (and in a free country it could not be otherwise), the United States has more doctors per capita than almost any other nation in the Western world. The government's own studies find that typically a family is no more than 20 minutes away from a doctor, a clinic, or a hospital. Public opinion polls indicate that an overwhelming number of Americans are satisfied with the care they receive.

Passage 3

One of the most bitterly attacked tax loopholes is that surrounding so-called business expenses. If an executive flies to the Super Bowl, he simply alleges that he had business in the city that played host to the Super Bowl. As a result of such a claim, the executive can deduct his Super Bowl expenses from his taxable income on the grounds that the trip was an expense incurred in his role as an agent of his employer.

An example of this outrage should make my point. A New York tax-payer claimed as a deduction $9,665 for business lunches in just 1 year. According to the man's records, he entertained a business client or associate on 338 different occasions. The taxpayer skipped his business lunch on Thanksgiving Day but not on the Friday, Saturday, or Sunday following. He entertained at top restaurants on an average of 6½ days a week all year at a cost of well over $20 for each lunch.

———————————————— SAMPLE RESPONSES ————————————————

Passage 1

CONCLUSION: *Materially, times are not bad.*

REASONS: *1. More households are affluent today.*
> *a. One in every 5 households in 1980 was affluent, with over $25,000 income. Twenty years ago, only 1 in 33 was this comfortable.*
> *2. Our personal income, disposable income, and personal savings have all climbed since 1950.*
>> *a. Fewer Americans—1 in every 8 rather than 1 in every 5—are below the poverty level. In 7 years, more than 14 million of us have climbed out of poverty.*
>> *b. While population has increased 56 percent, home ownership has increased 100 percent, car ownership 130 percent, and personal savings 696 percent between 1950 and 1980.*

First, let's look at reason 1. The writer compares ratios—1 in 5 versus 1 in 33. Is this comparison legitimate? No. A very important piece of information has been omitted. What income was needed to be affluent 20 years ago? He has failed to take inflation into account. Using this same logic, probably only 1 in 1,000 would have been comfortable 50 years ago.

The first part of the evidence for reason 2 suffers from the same problem. This evidence cannot be judged until we know how *poverty level* is defined. If the definition has not taken inflation into account or has changed in its basic meaning over time, then these ratios cannot be legitimately compared. Also, in reason 2a, the writer has tossed out an impressively large number—14 million. What percentage does that reflect? Has he taken population growth into account?

Reason 2b presents impressive percentage differences, but what do those percentages mean? Percentages of what? For example, is the home ownership figure based on the percentage of people who own homes, or on the absolute number of homes owned? To judge these percentages, we need to know how they were figured and the absolute numbers they were based upon.

While population has increased 56 percent, what has been the increase in numbers of families or potential homebuyers?

Without the omitted information, the evidence presented does not adequately support the conclusion.

Passage 2

Passage 2 can be outlined in the following manner:

CONCLUSION: *Health services in America are not so poor that government intrusion is imperative.*

REASONS: *1. Since 1970, infant mortality has dropped 30 percent, life expectancy has risen by a year, and nine of the leading causes of death have declined.*
2. The U.S. has more doctors per capita than almost any other nation in the Western world; typically a family is no more than 20 minutes away from a doctor.
3. Public opinion polls indicate that an overwhelming number of Americans are satsified with the care they receive.

To evaluate this use of evidence, we should first ask ourselves, What would be the most appropriate evidence to address the question, "Are health services in America poor?" You should immediately see that the definition of "poor" becomes crucial to deciding whether the statistics presented reflect "tricks" or not. If "good health services" is defined as adequate coverage available to everyone, at a cost that is not an excessive burden on one's income, then statistics about the infant mortality rate and the number of doctors do not prove that we have good health services. The more relevant statistics become those dealing with equity of access to such service, such as the cost of the services and the ability of various income groups to handle the financial burdens of these services. Note also that in Reason 1 there is no mention of the absolute infant mortality rate. Perhaps the U.S., even with the 30 percent drop, still has a higher rate than that in other countries.

Passage 3

CONCLUSION: *The business expense tax deduction is an outrage.*

REASON: *The deduction is unfair, and this inequity can be shown by the example of one New York taxpayer who claimed that his business activities required him to entertain at top restaurants an average of 6½ days per week all year long.*

While a single dramatic example illustrates potential abuse, it is not adequate evidence to support the generalization of widespread abuse. We have no way of knowing whether the example is typical.

Passage 4

How can those who attack busing claim that they are not motivated by racism? Private academies bus their students at least as much as the public schools where busing is required. Parents must not be sending their children to private academies to avoid long bus rides. A recent study of ten private academies for white students showed that private academies in the South bused more students farther than did public schools in the same region. The study found that public schools in the six states bused less than 50 percent of their students, while the academies bused an average of 60 percent. In addition, the average distance traveled by bus in the public schools was 8 miles per day, and in the private academies the comparable figure was 18 miles per day. Is it busing or integration that is being attacked?

X

How Good Is the Evidence: Are There Alternative Causal Explanations?

In the previous two chapters, your concern was with how well evidence supports generalizations. You learned questions that should be asked about all generalizations. In this chapter, you will learn questions to ask about a particular kind of generalization—a *causal generalization*. When you encounter such generalizations, it is necessary to ask special critical questions. This chapter focuses on these.

◊   *Critical Question:* **Are there alternative causal explanations?**

Different Levels of Generalization

Examine the two following groups of statements.

1a. Most sorority members use makeup.
1b. Sorority members are more likely to use makeup than nonsorority members.
1c. Joining a sorority causes college coeds to use more makeup.

2a. Few people who regularly jog have heart attacks.
2b. The more one jogs, the less likely one is to have a heart attack.
2c. The physical exercise provided by jogging tends to reduce the rate of heart attack.

First note that all these statements are generalizations. They are not simply statements about a few specific cases, but instead are about large groups of cases—namely sorority members and joggers. Second, note that the initial assertions in both groups of statements (1a and 2a) refer to characteristics of a *single group*; no comparisons are made. This is the simplest form of generalization. Such a generalization tells you that if you know someone who belongs to a group, you can determine the likelihood that she will have the characteristic. For example, 1a tells you that if a coed belongs to a sorority, she probably uses makeup.

The second assertions in each group of statements (1b and 2b) present *comparisons*; they refer to characteristics of *two* groups. In 1b, the use of makeup is compared for sorority and nonsorority members. In 2b, rate of heart attacks is compared for different rates of jogging activity. Comparisons permit us to determine *relationships*. If sorority members differ from nonsorority members in their use of makeup, a relationship exists between female group membership and makeup use. When knowing one thing (for example, sorority membership) helps us to predict another (for example, use of makeup), a predictive relationship exists. You will frequently encounter such statements of relationship. Here are a few:

> People who smoke cigarettes are more likely to get cancer than are those who do not smoke cigarettes.
>
> Intelligence scores are related to school performance.
>
> The more wealthy one is, the more likely one is to vote Republican.

Writers frequently jump from statements about relationships to statements claiming that one thing *causes* another. For example, 1c and 2c above are *causal* generalizations. Look carefully at how they differ from 1b and 2b. It is very easy to move from thinking about relationships to thinking about causes. It is often too easy! *The presence of a relationship between two things does not prove that one causes the other.* Only special kinds of evidence provide such proof. The major difficulty in proving causation is that two characteristics can be related for more than one reason. For example, it may be true that more sorority members than nonsorority members wear makeup, which indicates a relationship. This does not necessarily mean that belonging to a sorority *causes* one to wear more makeup. The relationship may reflect the fact that young women who tend to select sororities also tend to be the type of women who wear makeup.

Jumping from predictive relationships to causal inferences is a very common error. As a critical reader, you should always keep in mind that there are many reasons why one kind of condition or event may occur with another. Proving causal conclusions is much more difficult than proving the existence of a relationship. When writers make causal statements, always ask, Are there alternative reasons for why those events go together?

Causal Generalizations

Let's look more closely at what someone is concluding when she makes an inference about causation. What exactly is meant when someone says, "Joining a sorority causes college coeds to use more makeup," "TV violence causes aggressive behavior in children," or "There is a *causal link* between eating too much salt and high blood pressure"? The word *cause* means to bring about, make happen, or effect. Note the difference between the phrases *bring about* (causal) and *go together* (relationship). There are a number of words that will indicate to you when an author is thinking causally. We have listed a few.

> has the effect of
> increases the likelihood
> facilitates
> deters
> as a result of

There is another important aspect of *most* causal generalizations: They are probabilistic. Knowing one event does not tell you *for sure* whether the other event will occur. For example, if watching TV violence has the effect of *increasing the probability* of a child's being aggressive, then watching TV is a causal factor in aggressive behavior—even though many children who watch TV do not behave aggressively. If 25 percent of children who watch TV violence behave aggressively, and only 20 percent of children who don't watch such violence behave aggressively, then watching TV violence is probably one causal factor in aggressive behavior—even though most children who watch TV violence do not behave aggressively. If the *average* score on an exam increases *as a direct result of* students' drinking coffee, then drinking coffee is a causal factor, even though all students who drink coffee do not improve their exam scores.

In thinking about causation, you should also keep in mind that the probability of certain events' occurring is determined by many causal factors. For instance, TV violence may be only one of a number of factors causally linked to childhood aggression. Parental discipline, nutrition, genetic makeup, and peer group pressures may all be additional causal factors in determining aggressive behavior.

When writers make causal claims, they usually are not suggesting that the causal variable is the only factor causing the event—that is, they are not claiming that one factor is *necessary* for another to occur, nor that an effect will *necessarily occur* if the causal agent is present. Smoking may be a causal factor in cancer; yet many people who smoke may not get cancer, and many people who get cancer will not have smoked. Thus, most causes are only *contributory causes*; they are important factors among a number of factors. They increase the likelihood that an event will occur. Do not make the mistake of thinking that, because a factor is only one of several causes, it therefore is not an important one.

The Concept of Control—Ruling Out Alternative Reasons

A frequent sequence of causal thinking is as follows: Relationships are discovered, then someone offers a suggestion about what factor or factors might have caused the relationship—that is, someone makes a causal inference. If the findings could be due to other events besides the suggested cause, then the causal generalization is greatly weakened. So as a critical reader, you will want to search for alternative causes that might explain the results being discussed.

The careful researcher anticipates such a search and will try to isolate the causal factor of interest form other factors that might bring about the same effect. She will do this by using *controls*. A control is a process that helps rule out alternative reasons for effects. The concept of control will be more meaningful to you as the remainder of this chapter evolves. If you can come up with alternative reasons for an effect, an important control has been omitted. Omitting important controls seriously weakens reasoning.

In this section, we will examine some typical ways in which evidence is provided to support causal claims and indicate what controls are missing. In these illustrations we will focus on the question, Does eating food additives increase the likelihood that hyperactive children will have behavior problems? Several types of studies provide relevant causal generalizations, and each will be discussed in terms of the quality of its controls. Let's look at one type.

> Fifty hyperactive children who had taken large amounts of food additives were observed in their homes by trained raters who assessed the presence or absence of behavior problems. These raters found that 60 percent have behavior problems. The researcher concluded that food additives cause behavior problems in hyperactive children.

Can you tell from the data provided whether a causal relationship exists between taking food additives and having behavior problems? No. You do not know the rate of behavior problems in hyperactive children who have *not* eaten food additives. What if that rate is 70 percent? The researcher has failed to show the rate of the problem when the alleged causal factor was *absent*. One cannot show the effect of a "treatment" or a causal agent by studying only the group exposed to the treatment. In other words, there is no control for the typical rate of behavior problems among hyperactive children not taking food additives. The researcher, in effect, has not even demonstrated a relationship.

Let's look at another example of this type of reasoning.

> Being on the cover of *Sports Illustrated* is not a jinx. Researchers found that football and basketball teams that had been on the cover won their next game 70 percent of the time.

But what would their record have been if they had *not* been on the cover? We don't know, but we ought to. If you guessed 50 percent, you probably guessed wrong. In fact, the winning percentage probably would have been very high, since teams that show up on the cover tend to be the best teams in the country.

Let's look at another approach to the problem, using a hypothetical case.

A large number of hyperactive children were systematically observed before and after eating food containing large amounts of additives. Before ingesting the additives, 30 percent of the children exhibited psychological problems; after doing so, 50 percent of them exhibited problems. On the basis of these data, the researcher concluded that food additives cause behavior problems.

The reasoning in this kind of study is as follows: Because something occurs at a different rate following an event (in this case, eating food additives), that intervening event caused the change in rate. Such reasoning is fallacious! Why? Because such a study has failed to isolate the factor of interest. Many other factors which could have caused the changes could have occurred during the time interval. Ask yourself, Are there any other possible explanations of these changes?

Now compare your list with ours:

1. Many events that took place during the time period that food additives were used could have accounted for the changes. The children may have entered school and become exposed to and stimulated by other active children. The children got older; maybe there is a tendency for hyperactivity to increase with age. Classroom structure may have changed.
2. Another factor is *measurement*. Maybe hyperactive problem behaviors were measured differently after the intervening time.
3. Also, the very fact of being evaluated at one time may have had an effect on the children; for example, they may have tried less hard to "be good" as they were observed the second time.

The above approach clearly fails to provide controls adequate to rule out important alternative causes. The main problem again is that there is only a single group; there is no comparison group to show what changes would have occurred without the treatment.

Let's look at one more example to illustrate the problems with this type of reasoning. It has been found that the crime rate in a major American city has decreased since more people have become involved in Transcendental Meditation (TM). Could you conclude that TM has helped reduce the rate of crime? No, you couldn't. There are many alternative reasons for the change. For example, that city may also have doubled the size of its police force during the same time. In other words, the person conducting the study failed to control for the size of the city's police force.

A better method is to compare two groups that are identical in all important respects, except the causal factor of interest. However, the two-group method needs to be applied carefully to rule out alternative explanations. Let's examine a two-group comparison study.

> A researcher observed 50 hyperactive children who had eaten food additives and a group of 50 who had not eaten additives, and compared the rate of problem behaviors. Of those who had eaten additives, 50 percent showed behavior problems; of those who had not, 30 percent showed behavior problems.

Because there are two groups, this design permits one to decide whether or not a predictive relationship exists. The second group acts as a control for the typical rate of problem behaviors. In this case, there is a relationship between eating food additives and problem behaviors; the rate of problems was higher for those who had eaten food additives. But one cannot conclude that eating food additives is the cause. Why? Because subjects were not randomly assigned to the groups. It is therefore quite possible that the groups are not identical in important aspects, and these differences might account for the relationship. For example, the groups might differ in age, mental health of the parents, economic status of the parents, or kinds of food they eat. Any one of these factors might account for the differences in the rate of problem behaviors found. For example, older hyperactive children in general may show fewer behavior problems. If the second group were made up of older children, then the differences might be due to age factors, not additives. Because subjects are not randomly assigned, this design fails to rule out important alternative explanations. It has one important control procedure—the comparison group—but it fails to control for differences in the makeup of the groups.

Let's illustrate further.

> A researcher recently found that college students who had compatible roommates (group 1) had higher grade point averages than college students who didn't have compatible roommates (group 2).

Can we conclude that having a compatible roommate facilitates school achievement? No. There are obvious alternative factors that have not been ruled out. Can you think of some?

Since roommates are not randomly assigned to groups, isn't it quite possible that "brighter" students may have selected more compatible roommates to begin with? If so, group 1 would differ from group 2 in intelligence as well as in compatibility of roommates. Thus, the differences found could be due to differences in intelligence, not to differences in compatibility of roommates.

Always be especially cautious when researchers compare different groups as they *naturally exist*, rather than *randomly assigning* subjects to groups. The groups will almost always differ in important ways, and thus it will be impossible to isolate the effect of a single causal factor. For example, it might be misleading to compare achievement levels of children in open classrooms with achievement levels of children in traditional classrooms (the children in the open classrooms could be brighter). As another example, it could be misleading to compare the performance of the economic systems of two different societies (the two societies might differ in the accessibility of natural resources).

Even with control groups and random assignment, one has to examine a study carefully to see if all alternative causal factors have been ruled out. For example, *expectations* are frequently an important factor to control for. That is why when a Stopache Aspirin treatment group is compared to a no-aspirin control group, it is important that the no-aspirin group should think it is getting some curative agent, even though it only gets sugar pills. Subjects' expectations that they will get better may actually cause them to get better. The importance of expectations is why placebos are given in many studies. Placebos are inactive agents given as though they were actually active, in order to control for the effects of expectations. Remember to be on the lookout for the effects of expectations even when a study is well designed. Ask yourself, Would this study have benefited from including a group who received placebos?

It is impossible to discuss all the controls needed for adequate research. However, it is important for you to be on guard. When people make causal claims, always ask, Are there alternative factors that could have caused the results? If there are, such causal claims should be seriously questioned. Be especially wary when (a) subjects are not randomly assigned and (b) no comparison group is studied.

Correlation and Causation

There are often practical difficulties in randomly assigning subjects to different treatment groups. Consider, for example, the difficulties in randomly assigning parents to divorced versus nondivorced groups to study the effects of divorce on children. Thus, researchers frequently carry out what is usually called a *correlational study*. They collect two measures on each person belonging to a single group of people and see whether the two scores go together in a systematic way. For example, in studying the effects of food additives, a correlational research strategy might involve observing 50 third-grade children and rating each of them in two ways: (a) amount of food additives taken daily and (b) severity of behavior problems—perhaps rated from 1 (no problem) to 7 (serious problem). If these ratings go together systematically, then the characteristics measured are said to be *correlated*. For example, if severity of problem behavior increases whenever amount of food additives increases, a positive correlation can be said to exist.

Correlations are typically expressed as *correlation coefficients*—numbers ranging from +1.00 to −1.00. The closer the coefficient is to zero, the lower the correlation. Finding a significant correlation coefficient tells a researcher that a score on one factor can be predicted from knowledge of the score on the other. The ability to predict, however, is rarely perfect. In fact, when two characteristics are correlated, there is usually a great deal of error in predicting one from the other. The lower the correlation, the greater the error in prediction.

Two characteristics can be correlated for at least four reasons. The following example illustrates. It has been found that the warmer the personality of a psychotherapist, the more successful he is at psychotherapy; that is, there is a significant correlation between warmth (X) and success in psychotherapy (Y).

REASON 1: *X is a contributory cause of Y.* (Warmth is indeed a causal factor.)

REASON 2: *Y is a contributory cause of X.* (Therapists who are successful become warmer toward their patients.)

REASON 3: *X and Y interact.* (Warmth is *sometimes* the cause of success, and success is sometimes the cause of warmth.)

REASON 4: *Both X and Y are effects of a third factor.* (Perhaps people who are intelligent tend to be both warm and successful. If so, warmth and success will correlate because of how they both relate to intelligence.)

Examine the following correlational finding: Researchers have found a correlation between the number of mystery novels males read and the frequency of wife abuse. Which of the four previously listed reasons might explain such results? Can you see alternative explanations for the findings? We will mention one to get you started. Perhaps men who have violent personality tendencies tend to read mystery novels and also tend to beat their wives.

Fallacies in Causal Reasoning

Because there are a number of reasons that characteristics might go together, it is always fallacious to assume that because two events go together, or because two characteristics are correlated, one is the cause and the other is the effect. We will refer to this fallacy of making causal inferences on the basis of concurrent events as the *false-cause* fallacy. Watch for this fallacy. It is very common.

You will frequently see false-cause reasoning in reports that do not include formal correlational results but simply argue that because event B *followed* event A, B caused A. This flawed form of causal reasoning is commonly called the *post hoc, ergo propter hoc* (after this, therefore because of this) *fallacy*, or, for short, the *post hoc fallacy*. The following examples illustrate the problem with this kind of reasoning.

"Harry Hurricane must be an excellent coach; since he moved to our university, the team's record has improved dramatically." (But maybe the university also decided to double its athletic budget when Harry came.) "This reduction of the speed limit has really cut down the accident rate; 20 percent fewer fatalities have occurred this year." (But maybe cars were also built more safely.) Politicians are especially fond of the post hoc argument: "Since I have been in office, inflation has decreased to a 4 percent level," or, "Following our party's tax reforms, the economy has really heated up."

Remember: The finding of a significant correlation, or the finding that one event follows another in time, does not by itself prove causation. When causal inferences are made from such data, the false-cause fallacy has been committed.

Practice Exercises

◊ *Critical Question:* **Are there alternative causal explanations?**

For each passage, evaluate the quality of the generalization by examining the quality of the evidence used to support it.

Passage 1

A research analyst studied murder statistics for 32 states between 1975 and 1985, a decade when the murder rate was rising nationally and the number of executions was declining.

He measured what happened to murder rates in states that abolished the death penalty before 1975, in those that still had a death penalty law but carried out few executions, and in those that used the law more frequently until court decisions forced an end to capital punishment.

He wrote, "Capital punishment does not, on balance, deter homicides." If capital punishment deters murder, the murder rate should have increased the most in states where the risk of execution declined the most. Instead, the states that ended the death penalty had smaller increases in homicide rates.

Passage 2

Two drinks a day may be beneficial to your health. A 10-year study of more than 8,000 people in California found those who had two or fewer drinks a day had lower death rates than abstainers.

But the death rate was significantly higher for those who had six or more drinks of alcohol a day.

The findings indicate that moderate alcohol consumption may have a protective effect against heart disease. Four groups of people enrolled in the Kaiser-Permanente health plan were examined: those who did not drink, those who had two or fewer drinks a day, those who had three to five drinks daily, and those reporting six or more drinks a day.

Those imbibing two or fewer drinks a day had the lowest mortality rate. Death rates for nondrinkers were 40 percent higher than the rates for the lightest drinkers. Those drinking three to five drinks a day had a mortality rate 50 percent higher than the lighter drinkers. The heaviest drinkers had a doubled mortality rate.

Passage 3

Sixty students at the University of Wisdom recently agreed to participate in a program designed to improve their dating skills.

The students who volunteered for the program averaged one date during the month prior to their participation in the dating-skills program. The 60 students were divided into three groups: One group had six "practice" dates with six different volunteers; a second group also had six "practice" dates and received feedback from their dates concerning their appearance and behavior; a third group served as a control.

Before and after the practice dates, each group filled out social anxiety questionnaires and rated themselves in terms of social skills. Both of the two groups who had practice dates experienced less social anxiety, a higher sense of self-confidence in social situations, and more dates than did the control group. Apparently, practice dating improves the quality of our social life.

--- **SAMPLE RESPONSES** ---

Passage 1

CONCLUSION: *Capital punishment does not deter homicide.*

REASON: *The states that ended the death penalty had smaller increases in homicide rates.*

The evidence for the causal generalization focuses on a 10-year comparison of homicide rates in 32 states with varying attitudes toward the death penalty. One positive characteristic of the study is the existence of multiple groups: states that abolished the death penalty before 1975, those that still had a death penalty law but carried out few executions, and those that used the law frequently until court decisions temporarily halted capital punishment (in 1978). A major weakness is that states were not randomly assigned to these groups. Thus, we should be especially alert to important differences among the groups of states. Do they differ in major ways other than in their use of capital punishment? For example, there is no evidence about the homicide rates in individual states *prior* to the period of the study. If these states with higher increases in homicide rates also traditionally have had higher than average rates of increase, then the comparison between groups is biased. The more relevant data would be the *within*-state homicide rates before and after change in the status of capital punishment. Perhaps those states with lower-than-average increases in homicide rates in the absence of capital punishment also had lower rates of increase during the period when they imposed capital punishment. In other words, another factor besides capital punishment may be responsible for the differences in homicide rate among states. Consequently, we cannot conclude that the evidence necessarily supports the generalization.

Passage 2

CONCLUSION: *Moderate alcohol consumption may protect against heart disease.*

REASON: *Death rates for nondrinkers were 40 percent higher than those for the lightest drinkers. Those in the three-to-five drinks a day group had a mortality rate 50 percent higher than the lighter drinkers. The heaviest drinkers had a doubled mortality rate.*

Though this research study used comparison groups, subjects could not be *randomly* assigned. Thus, there are likely to be other factors besides the alleged cause (drinking) that may have caused the differential heart-disease rates. We should ask, for example, whether the researchers controlled for age, sex, and smoking habits. Are there other ways in which light drinkers differ from nondrinkers and heavy drinkers? Perhaps they differ in weight or in lifestyle characteristics that might be related to the rate of heart disease. Without having a better idea of how else these groups might have differed, we can't have confidence in the generalization.

Passage 3

CONCLUSION: *Dating behavior of students will be improved by an increase in dating experience.*

REASON: *Forty students at the University of Wisdom reported increased dates, improved social skills, and less social anxiety after six practice dates compared to those of 20 control-group students.*

This study controlled for many important factors. However, the *expectations* of the participants in the study may have affected the results. Those who conducted the experiment apparently made no attempt to convince the students in the control group that their dating behavior would be improved. Consequently, although this study was quite well designed, we should have reservations about whether practice dating was the significant causal factor in determining changes in the quality of dating behavior.

Did you notice how "improved dating behavior" was measured here? Recalling what you learned in Chapter VIII, can you see any problems with this form of measurement?

Passage 4 (Self-Examination): Complex Passage

55 MPH[1]

Walter Isaacson

PRO. When a policy not only achieves its desired result, but also produces a fortuitous side effect, there is reason to celebrate. The federal law setting speed limits at 55 MPH represents one of those rare instances when the Law of Unintended Consequences actually works to our advantage. Not only does the law conserve energy, as it was supposed to, it also saves the lives of up to fifteen Americans every single day! No wonder more than 70 percent of the public, according to a 1980 Gallup Poll, support staying alive at 55.

The nationwide speed limit was enacted in 1974 in response to the oil embargo that almost crippled the nation. Its original purpose was fuel conservation. Cars operate more efficiently at 55 MPH than they do at higher speeds; depending on the size of the auto, it uses anywhere from 10 percent to 30 percent less gasoline to travel a certain distance at 55 MPH than at 70 MPH. Originally, the Department of Transportation estimated the annual savings at 1.5 billion gallons a year. But recent analysis, which takes into account the more efficient engines and lower gear ratios now used in cars and trucks, shows that the saving is even greater—approximately 3.4 billion gallons a year of gas being conserved solely because

[1]Reprinted by permission of the Putnam Publishing Group from PRO AND CON by Walter Isaacson. Copyright 1983 © by Walter Isaacson.

of the new speed limit. This is about 3 percent of our total national consumption of oil, a significant saving.

As a result, consumers in the United States save $4.6 billion a year on the amount they pay for gas. This is money that goes into our pockets, and not the bloated treasuries of the Organization of Petroleum Exporting Countries (OPEC). Besides saving money, the law improves our trade balance and strengthens our national security by making us less dependent on (and less beholden to the political pressures of) foreign sources of oil.

Even most trucking lines and bus companies support the law, despite the extra time it takes to move their cargo and passengers. Not only do they save on fuel, but they reduce maintenance costs. Consolidated Freightways, the motor cargo giant, has changed the gear ratios on their fleet to limit top speed to 57 MPH, cutting their gas guzzling by an additional 8 percent. United Parcel Service found that their trucks traveling at 55 MPH used 32 percent less fuel than the same ones when driven at 65 MPH.

During the first year that the law was in effect, traffic deaths decreased by 16 percent, saving 9,000 lives. Part of the lifesaving was due to the 2.3 percent drop in the number of miles people drove that year (due to the difficulty of getting gas). But the National Safety Council, after carefully examining the change in fatality rates in different situations, concluded that up to 59 percent of the lives saved were due to the lower speed limit. Nonfatal injuries during the first year of the lower nationwide speed limit also declined by about 200,000 cases, at least half of the drop due to the new law. Simple multiplication leads to the conclusion that there are now 1 million fewer people injured and 50,000 fewer people dead because the law existed from 1974 through 1983.

Roger Penske is a lifelong car racing enthusiast, both as a driver and now a team owner. He is also chairman of the Automobile Safety Foundation. Penske explains the safety factors involved in the lower speed limit: "If you have a crash at 70 MPH or faster, your chances of survival are 50–50. Cut your speed to between 50 and 60 MPH, and the odds climb to about 31–1 in your favor." In addition, the law tends to keep cars moving at a similar pace (the difference between the fast-moving cars and the slower ones is less), and thus one of the major causes of accidents, drivers weaving from lane to lane, is reduced.

Admittedly, some people tend to disobey the law. But when the speed limit was 70 MPH, people exceeded that too. According to Vincent Tofany, president of the National Safety Council, "The public has always violated a speed limit, no matter what it is, by 5 to 7 MPH." Department of Transportation surveys show that 85 percent of highway motorists now travel at 62 MPH or less, compared to the old limits when many drivers traveled at close to 80 MPH. Lowering the legal limit has greatly reduced the speed at which people actually drive.

It is hard to quantify precisely the annual costs and benefits that come from slowing down highway traffic. But Professors Charles Clotfelter and John Hahn, in a study published in *Policy Sciences* in 1978, tried to do just that. Using 1974 prices (when gasoline cost only 72 cents a gallon), their most conservative dollar estimates per year were:

Costs	*Benefits*
Added time on the road $2.9 billion	Gasoline saved $2.4 billion
Added police enforcement $800 million	Lives saved (at $240,000 per) $998 million
	Injuries averted $735 million
	Reduced property damage $236 million
Excess of benefits over costs: $1.5 billion.	

Clotfelter and Hahn conclude: "Even modest estimates of the benefits of the 55 MPH speed limit exceed the upper bound estimates of cost."

"All the evidence is favorable," says Penske. "The law saves gas. And lives." Adds Tofany: "What we're talking about is conserving energy, which clearly is in the national interest, and conserving a national resource—people."

CON. The double-nickel law is merely a symbolic gesture. The gas savings are insignificant. The reduction in fatalities comes at an inordinate cost and could be accomplished more efficiently. This federal law is an unwarranted infringement on the rights of states and individuals; its costs in terms of time and freedom lost are incalculable. "I think it's a stinking law," says Federal Highway Administrator Ray Barnhart. It should be repealed, just as the 1980 Republican platform promised.

Proponents of driving 55 have manipulated statistics to prove that it is an effective energy-conservation method. But *Road and Track* magazine did its own analysis. Taking into account that only one-third of driving is done on the highway, and that gasoline consumption is only a part of the country's total energy expenditure, it figured that the maximum savings from the 55 MPH limit "amount to less than one-half of one percent of total energy requirements." Another study, done by Professor Donald Rapp at the University of Texas and reported in *Consumer Research* magazine, estimated that the law saves only 1.3 percent of all petroleum used in the United States. Similar savings could come simply by ensuring that every driver kept his tires inflated properly!

Nor is it clear that the total number of lives saved is as high as the highway safety lobby estimates. Fatalities have fallen, but much of the reduction is to be found on city streets where the law is not relevant. And on interstates, it has been shown that keeping a constant speed of traffic flow is more important than forcing people to slow down. The reduction in accidents is mainly due to the fact that people are driving less and wearing seat belts more frequently. Indeed, when we look at traffic fatalities per mile driven, the sharp decline in deaths began with the rise in gas prices in 1973, and this ratio actually increased a bit in the first few months after the 1974 law went into effect.

Undoubtedly, there are some benefits from lowering the speed limit to 55 MPH. These benefits would be even greater if the limit were lowered to 50 MPH, or even 40 MPH. But it is imperative to realize the costs of such actions. In choosing the speed best suited for highway travel—which could be set at anywhere from, say, 40 MPH to 80 MPH—the goal should be to find the best ratio of benefits to cost. Putting a dollar value on benefits and costs is difficult, but it can be done.

The greatest cost by far, one that has been underestimated by people such as Clotfelter and Hahn, is the added time spent on the road due to the lower limit. Each of us who must travel bears that burden, as do all people who depend on food, commodities, and business products that must be transported. This, of course, includes everybody. Time is money.

Charles Lave, a professor of economics and a member of the Institute of Transportation Studies at the University of California at Irvine, reported on his calculations in *Newsweek*. The new speed limit caused an increase in the total amount of driving time in the United States of 2.7 million hours a year. Lave uses a standard "preference evaluation" that shows that people are willing to pay 42 percent of an hour's wage to save an hour of driving time. "When we do this," he says, "we find that the 55 MPH limit causes enough of a traffic slowdown to waste about $6 billion worth of travel time per year."

Assuming 4500 fewer fatalities a year, each life saved thus costs the country $1.3 million. Critics of this kind of cost analysis may argue that any life is worth saving no matter what it costs, but Lave points out other expenditures that could save comparable numbers of lives. Installing smoke detectors in every home would save just as many people, at a cost of only about $80,000 per life saved. Additional mobile cardiac units would cost only around $2000 per life. Resources are not infinite; decisions about cost-effectiveness must be made.

The 55 MPH limit is expensive in other ways. Setting a national speed limit is an usurpation by the federal government of a power that historically has belonged to the states. In the wide-open states of the West, where traffic conditions on the endless ribbons of road are much different than in the

East, the nationwide standard causes particular hardship. Says Wyoming State Senator Cal Taggart, who is leading the fight to raise the limit: "For those of us in the West, it takes forever to get from here to there." That is why Nevada has flouted the law by setting a token $5 fine for violators. "Here it's not like one of those eastern states where the population density is so much greater and it's maybe 55 miles from one end of the state to the other," says Las Vegas driver Dennis Gomes. "I would rather have a little risk and get to where I'm going faster."

Gomes's sentiment raises a sticky public policy issue: What trade-offs should be made between individual liberties and public benefits? Saving gas and lives is a legitimate public goal, but forcing people to drive slower than is natural and reasonable is a restriction of freedom. Both factors must be balanced in the equation before setting policy. In the case of the 55 MPH law, the public benefits clearly do not outweigh the costs and thus do not justify regulating individual conduct in a way that provokes a disrespect for and disobedience of the law.

Now that the gasoline crisis has eased and the threat to national security is not as pressing, the costly and unreasonable 55 MPH limit should be lifted. Efforts should be spent on making cars more fuel efficient and safer. The futile and symbolic gesture hastily made in 1974 should not burden our country forever.

MOTOR VEHICLE DEATHS

Year	Total	Per 100 Million Miles Driven
1973	55,500	4.1
1974	46,400	3.5
1975	45,900	3.4
1976	47,000	3.3
1977	49,500	3.3
1978	52,400	3.3
1979	52,800	3.3
1980	52,600	3.3
1981	50,700	3.2

SOURCE: National Safety Council

DOMESTIC GASOLINE CONSUMPTION

Year	Billions of Gallons	Gallons per Vehicle
1973	110.5	851
1974	106.3	788
1975	109.0	790
1976	115.7	807
1977	119.6	804
1978	125.1	813
1979	122.1	765
1980	115.0	711

SOURCE: Federal Highway Administration

XI

Are There
Any Errors
in Reasoning?

In the previous three chapters, you learned what questions to ask to decide how well evidence supports a generalization. You focused on arguments in which generalizations were the conclusion, and evidence was the reason—that is, generalization arguments. When you answer the question, How good is the evidence?, in a generalization argument, you have finished most of your evaluation task, since all that is left to decide is whether or not to believe the generalization. However, in more complex arguments, examining the evidence is just a beginning. Let's see why, by taking a look at the following brief argument:

> The government should subsidize sugar growers. If American sugar farmers are unable to meet production costs, they will be forced to quit growing sugar, and we will be entirely dependent upon foreign sources. Besides, sugar farmers are making lower profits today than they were 10 years ago.

First, note that there is no statistical evidence. Two generalizations are used to support a prescription. Many arguments contain one or a series of factual claims either to support another factual claim or to support a prescriptive conclusion. This type of structure requires you to focus on two problems: (a) Are the supporting reasons true?, and (b) If so, does the conclusion logically follow from them? To answer question (a), you first apply the questions you learned to ask in Chapters VIII to X. How good is the evidence for the supporting reasons? How much can we trust the source of the assertion? To answer the second question, closely examine the logic of the reasoning used to arrive at the conclusion. To do this, you must evaluate assumptions. Bad assumptions make for bad reasoning.

We refer to bad reasoning as an *error in reasoning*, which we define as any example of reasoning that involves erroneous or incorrect assumptions.

↷   *Critical Question:*   **Are there any errors in reasoning?**

Truth and Validity

If particular reasons require erroneous assumptions to link them to the conclusion, then obviously the conclusion will not be supported by such reasons. When you find this situation, you have found an example of *invalid reasoning*. *Valid reasoning*, as we will use the term, is reasoning in which the assumption linking one statement to another appears to be highly probable. In arguments other than generalization arguments, you must judge both the *truth of the reasons* and the *validity of the reasoning*. Thus, a reason can be true at the same time that the reasoning is invalid. The following example illustrates:

> We should not allow capital punishment. Britain does not permit capital punishment, and its homicide rate is much lower than ours.

Now assume that the reason is true. The conclusion only follows if it is assumed that Britain and the United States are not different in many important dimensions related to the homicide rate. Such an assumption is unwarranted; thus, the reasoning is of questionable validity.

Note that a conclusion is not necessarily wrong because the reasoning is invalid. In such a case, the conclusion simply is not supported by that particular reason or pattern of reasoning.

Evaluating Assumptions

If you have been able to locate assumptions (see Chapters VI and VII), you already have the major skills for finding errors in reasoning. The more questionable the assumption, the more erroneous the reasoning. Some reasoning will involve descriptive assumptions that you will want to agree or disagree with on the basis of other facts you may be aware of. Some reasoning will be so irrelevant to the conclusion that you would have to supply blatantly erroneous assumptions to provide a logical link. You should immediately reject such reasoning. Some reasoning will involve value assumptions, and you will have to use your own personal value preferences as a guide to evaluating them.

To demonstrate the process you should go through to evaluate assumptions, we will examine the quality of the reasoning in the following passage. We will begin by assembling the structure.

> The question involved in this legislation is a critical one. It is not really a question of whether cigarette smoking is or is not deterimental to health. Rather it is a question of whether Congress is willing for the Federal Communications Commission to make an arbitrary decision that prohibits cigarette advertising on radio and television. If we should permit the FCC to take this action in regard to cigarette smoking, what is there to prevent them from deciding next year that candy is detrimental to the public health in that it causes obesity, tooth decay, and other health problems? What about milk and eggs? Milk and eggs are high in saturated animal fat and no doubt increase the cholesterol in the bloodstream, believed by many heart specialists to be a contributing factor in heart disease. Do we want the FCC to be able to prohibit the advertising of milk, eggs, butter, and ice cream on TV?
>
> We all know that no action by the federal government, however drastic, can or will be effective in eliminating cigarette smoking completely. National prohibition of alcoholic beverages was attempted, but the Eighteenth Amendment, after only 14 years of stormy existence, was repealed by the Twenty-first.

CONCLUSION: *The FCC should not prohibit cigarette advertising on radio and television.*

REASONS: 1. *If we permit the FCC to prohibit advertising on radio and television, the FCC will soon prohibit many kinds of advertising, since many products present potential health hazards.*
2. *No action by the federal government can or will be effective in eliminating cigarette smoking completely. National prohibition of alcohol didn't work.*

First, the truth of the first reason depends upon an underlying assumption that once we allow actions to be taken on the merits of one case, it will be more difficult to stop actions on similar cases. We do not agree with this assumption, mainly because we believe that there are plenty of steps in our legal system to prevent such actions if they appear unjustified. Thus, we judge this reason to be untrue.

The credibility of the second reason is questionable because of the weak evidence—an exciting example out of the past. Even if this reason were true, we disagree with an assumption linking the reason to the conclusion, the assumption that the major goal of prohibiting cigarette advertising on radio and television is to *eliminate cigarette smoking completely.* A more likely goal is to *reduce consumption.* Thus we judge this reason to be weakly supported, and judge the reasoning connecting the reason to the conclusion as having questionable validity.

As you search for errors in reasoning, *always keep the conclusion in mind;* then ask yourself, What reasons would be adequate to support this position? If there is a large difference between the reasons presented and what you believe to be strong reasons, there is likely to be an error in reasoning. A further hint we can give you is that, typically, when individuals are claiming that one *action* is more desirable than another, strong reasons will refer to the advantages or disadvantages of adopting a particular position. When reasoning strays from advantages and disadvantages, be especially watchful for errors in reasoning.

Common Reasoning Errors

There are numerous common reasoning errors. Many are so common that they have been given fancy names. Fortunately, it is not necessary for you to be aware of all the common reasoning errors and their names to be able to locate them. If you ask yourself the right questions, you will be able to find reasoning errors—even if you can't name them. Thus, we have adopted the strategy of emphasizing self-questioning strategies, rather than of asking you to memorize an extensive list of possible kinds of errors.

We are now going to take you through some exercises in discovering common reasoning errors. Once you know how to look, you will be able to find most errors. In Exercise A, do the following: First, identify the conclusion and reason. Second, determine whether the reason states an advantage or a disadvantage. Third, identify any necessary assumptions by asking yourself, If the reason were true, what would one have to believe for it to logically support the conclusion, and what does one have to believe for the reason to be true? Last, ask yourself, Do these assumptions make sense? If an obviously erroneous assumption is being made, you have found an error in reasoning, and that reasoning can be judged invalid.

EXERCISE A

Fluorine is the most toxic chemical on earth; it is so powerful in its corrosive effect that it is used to etch glass. The idea of putting that sort of chemical into our drinking water is just insane. Fluoridation is a menace to health.

Additionally, many medical associations are opposed to fluoridation. For instance, the Texas Medical Association declined to recommend it.

It's not hard to explain why some doctors favor fluoridation. For instance, one of its leading advocates has been Dr. Danger, Dean and Research Professor of Nutrition at the State University Medical School. In the past 6 years, Dr. Danger received over $350,000 from the food processors, the refined-sugar interests, the soft-drink people, and the chemical and drug interests. Every true nutritionist knows that it is refined sweets, soft drinks, and refined flour that are the basic causes of defective teeth. Is it any wonder that the processors of these foods are so active in helping the chemical interests to cover up for them?

As a first step in analyzing for fallacies, let's outline the argument.

CONCLUSION: *Drinking water should not be fluoridated.*

REASONS: *1. Fluoridation is the most dangerous toxic chemical on earth; it is so powerful in its corrosive effect that it is used to etch glass.*
2. Many medical associations are opposed to fluoridation. a. The Texas Medical Association declined to recommend it.
3. Some doctors personally benefit by endorsing fluoridation. Dr. Danger received large sums of money from business groups during the time he endorsed fluoridation.

In the first paragraph, the author tries to prove that fluoridation is very dangerous—a disadvantage. He does this by stating that fluorine is the most toxic chemical on earth; it is so powerful in its corrosive effect that it is used to etch glass. What erroneous assumptions are being made? First, note that the author used *fluorine* to prove something about *fluoridation*. A dictionary will quickly show you that fluorine is not the same as fluoride. The writer has shifted words on us. One cannot assume that fluorine and fluoride have the same effect; nor can one assume that any such chemicals when in diluted form will behave as they do in undiluted form. Thus, there is no proof here that fluoridation is dangerous—only that fluorine, in undiluted form, is dangerous. This erroneous reasoning is an example of equivocation, discussed in Chapter VI.

Now, carefully examine the author's second argument. What assumptions are being made? To prove that fluoridation is bad, he appeals to a personal testimonial; he thus moves away from pointing out factual advantages or disadvantages of fluoridation. Recall that personal testimonials are insufficient proof. A position is not bad just because authorities are against it. What is important in determining the validity of such reasoning is the evidence that the authorities are using in making their judgment.

In addition, in this second argument the writer shifts words on us again. He argues that many medical associations "are opposed to" fluoridation and supports this with the fact that the Texas Medical Association "declined to recommend" it. Does *decline to recommend* mean the same as *oppose*? No—*oppose* implies definite disapproval; *decline to recommend* simply signifies an unwillingness to approve. Additionally, is the Texas Medical Association representative of medical associations in general?

What about the third paragraph? Has the writer pointed out advantages or disadvantages of fluoridation? No. He has basically tried to prove that Dr. Danger is biased in his viewpoint. He has attacked Dr. Danger, who favors fluoridation; he has not attacked the issue. He has not proven anything about the benefits or dangers of fluoridation. Even if Dr. Danger is biased, his views on fluoridation may still be correct. The issue is whether or not fluoridation is desirable, not whether Dr. Danger is an ethical person. *One does not prove a point by attacking a person*. The assumption that because a person may have undesirable qualities, his ideas are therefore undesirable is clearly a bad assumption. Such an argument diverts attention from the issue. A good argument attacks ideas, not the person with the ideas. Attacking a person, rather than ideas, is frequently called an *ad hominem* argument.

Now, we will look at an argument favoring fluoridation.

EXERCISE B

> Fluoridation is opposed by a crackpot, antiscientific minority. I do not
> believe that a minority ever has the right to keep the majority from
> getting what they want. In any city where a majority of us want fluor-
> idation, we should have it; that is the democratic way.

First, let's again keep the structure of the argument in mind as we search for errors. Also, let's once again ask whether the author has strayed from discussing the advantages and disadvantages of fluoridation.

Clearly, the author has not focused on the advantages and disadvantages. First, what do you think about the phrase "crackpot, antiscientific minority"? Obviously, he is giving his opponents a bad name. This is a common problem referred to as *name calling*. For this reason to support the conclusion, it must be assumed that if a group can be labeled with negative adjectives, then their ideas are erroneous. Wrong! Even if opponents of fluoridation deserve their bad name, it is still very possible that fluoridation *is* a bad thing, according to the *facts*. Be wary of name calling!

What about the argument that we ought to do what the majority wants? Certainly it sounds very democratic. But what assurance do we have that the majority are basing their judgments on the *appropriate evidence*? What if there were evidence available that fluoridation caused cancer, but the majority continued to ignore the evidence? We think you get the point. There is no substitute for the facts. Be wary of phrases like, "Most Americans agree that . . ." or "Everybody knows that . . . ." These phrases represent appeals to group-approved attitudes and are frequently referred to as *ad populum* arguments. Again, note that such arguments divert attention from the real issue.

Now let's examine some arguments related to another controversy: Should Congress approve a federally funded child development program which would provide day-care centers for children?

EXERCISE C

I am against the government's child development program. First, I am interested in protecting the children of this country. They need to be protected from social planners and self-righteous ideologues who would disrupt the normal course of life and tear them from ther mothers and families to make them pawns in a univeral scheme designed to produce infinite happiness in 20 years. Children should grow up with their mothers, not with a series of caretakers and nurses' aides.

What is at issue is whether parents shall continue to have the right to form the characters of their children, or whether the State with all its power should be given the tools and techniques for forming the young.

Let's again begin by outlining the argument.

CONCLUSION: *I am against the government's child-development program.*

REASONS: *1. Our children need to be protected from social planners and self-righteous ideologues, who would disrupt the normal course of life and tear them from their families.*
2. The parents, not the State, should have the right to form the characters of their children.

As critical readers, we should be looking for specific facts about the program. Do you find any specifics in the first reason? No. The reason is saturated with undefined and emotionally loaded generalities. We have underlined a couple of these terms. Such terms will typically generate negative emotions, which the writer hopes the reader will associate with the position she is attacking. Again, the writer is engaging in name calling. The use of emotionally charged negative terms serves to distract the reader from the facts.

The writer has tricked us in another way. He states that the program will "tear them from their families and mothers," and the children will be "pawns in a universal scheme." Of course, nobody wants these things to happen to their children. However, the important question is whether *in fact* the bill will do these things. Not likely! The writer is playing two common tricks on us. First, he is appealing to our emotions with his choice of words. Second, he has set up a position to attack which in fact does not exist, making it much easier to get the reader on his side. He has *extended* the opposition's position to an "easy-to-attack" position. The erroneous assumption in this case is that the position attacked is the same as the position actually presented in the legislation. The lesson for the critical thinker is, When someone attacks aspects of a position, always check to see if he is fairly representing the position. If not, you have located the *extension* error. The best way to check how fairly a position is being represented is to get the facts about all positions.

Let's now look closely at the second reason. The writer states that either the parents shall have the right to form the characters of their children, or else the State should be given the decisive tools. For statements like this to be true, one must asume that there are only two choices. Are there? No! The writer has created a *false dilemma.* Isn't it possible for the child development program to exist and also for the family to have a significant influence on the child? Always be cautious when controversies are treated as if only two choices are possible; there are frequently more than two. When a writer oversimplifies an issue by stating only two choices, the error is referred to as an *either–or* error. To find *either–or* errors, be on the alert for phrases like the following:

> either . . . or
> the only alternative is
> the two choices are
> since A has not worked, *only* B will

Let's shift to a different controversy: Should there be businesses that sell term papers to students?

EXERCISE D

What's wrong with buying term papers? Most students resort to buying them only because they realize that the system is rotten; the term paper itself has become a farce in the eyes of the students, since they are required to go through the mechanical motions, month after month, of putting things down tediously on paper, writing correct sentences, organizing their paragraphs and ideas, thinking up arguments to use, and all those rituals—surely you aren't going to claim that that is ed-ucation. Real education is ecstasy, the peak experience.[1]

---

[1]M.Beardsley, *Thinking Straight,* 4th ed. (Englewood Cliffs, N.J.: Prentice-Hall, 1975), pp. 237–38.

Again, let's start by outlining the argument.

CONCLUSION: *Buying term papers is defensible.*

REASON: *Term paper rituals are not education; real education is ecstasy, the peak experience.*

The major reason given is "proven" by the "fact" that "real education is ecstasy, the peak experience." Sounds good—but what does it mean? The writer has tried to seduce the reader by using showy terms that have an emotional appeal. He has provided us with glittering generalities, hoping that we will not require a more precise or specific definition of the goals of education and of the appropriate behaviors for obtaining such goals. A position is not good or bad because we can associate it with a good or bad label or a smug phrase. *Good reasons provide specifics!*

Be especially on the lookout for glib phrases or pet slogans. A few common ones follow:

> A woman's place is in the home.
> Nice guys finish last. (Always?)
> Vote for our party—we are for peace and prosperity. (Who isn't?)
> Human nature is unchangeable.
> Work is what made this country great.
> Moderation is everything.

Further Diversions

Emotional language is one way that writers and speakers divert our attention from the issue. There is another very common diversionary device. Let's take a look.

> I do not see why people think it is so important to the cause of women's rights that we adopt the Equal Rights Amendment. Why, just look at all the problems we are having with hiring enough women in universities. We hear stories all the time of women not wanting the jobs that are offered.

What is the real issue? Passing or not passing the ERA. But if you are not careful you will get involved in the question of whether there are enough qualified women for academic jobs rather than in the issue of the advantages and disadvantages of the ERA. The writer has diverted the reader's attention to another issue. When a writer or speaker does this, we can say that he has drawn a *red herring* across the trail of the argument. Red herring arguments are very common. Many of us are adept at these, as the following example illustrates:

> Mother: Why did you come home an hour late for dinner, when I told you to be on time?
>
> Daughter: You're always picking on me.

If the daughter is successful, the issue will become whether the mother is picking on her daughter, not why the daughter was out late.

You should normally have no difficulty spotting red herrings as long as you keep the real issue in mind as well as the kind of evidence needed to resolve it.

Faulty Analogy

Look closely at the structure of the following brief argument, paying special attention to the reason supporting the conclusion.

> Education cannot prepare men and women for marriage. Trying to educate them for marriage is like trying to teach them to swim without allowing them to go into the water. It cannot be done.

The reason is a statement about *resemblance*. The argument compares a specific case with a situation known through past experience—a form of argument we call *reasoning by analogy.* In essence, the structure of this reasoning is as follows: Since two things are like each other in some important way (in this case, both involve teaching a new skill), then if one has a further characteristic (for example, learning can only take place in the medium in which the skill will be used), the other will also have that characteristic.

On the surface, analogies frequently seem to provide compelling support for a conclusion. They capitalize on our ability to learn from the past. Analogies are sometimes useful devices for getting to the core of an argument. At other times they are deceptive persuasive devices. Let's take a close look at the structure of an argument from analogy.

> X has characteristics a, b, c.
> Y has characteristics a, b, c.
> X also has a further characteristic w.
> Therefore, Y has the characteristic w.

The conclusion does not necessarily follow. Let's see why. Learning to swim, the basis of the previous analogy, has characteristics in common with learning to be a marriage partner; for example, they both require learning some new skills. But they also have important *different* characteristics; for example, swimming requires primarily motor-coordination skills, whereas marriage requires primarily social-emotional skills. In fact, two different things will always have different characteristics, no matter how many characteristics they may have in common. Analogical arguments are weakened because of this, since the logic of analogical arguments demands that *all* significant characteristics be similar.

So what good is reasoning by analogy? Well, such reasoning can illuminate important hidden generalizations that we might not see otherwise, and that when found can then be applied to the argument. For example, the previous analogical argument suggests that everything that involves learning a new skill also requires learning it in the medium in which it will ultimately be used. The issue then becomes whether the generalization is true. In this case, evidence suggests that it is not entirely true. If it were, all education in the classroom would be irrelevant to the learning of skills used outside the classroom.

Thus, when you encounter an argument by analogy, first determine whether the two things being compared really do have something or a number of things in common and whether they differ in significant characteristics. If similarities seem to override differences, try to ascertain the hidden generalization and determine its truth. If they do not, reject the analogy as even illuminating and go on to more legitimate reasons.

Let's analyze the following argument from analogy in such a manner.

> I don't see what is wrong with the steel strike. After all, if someone came to your store and offered to pay you $1 for sugar that you were selling for $1.25, you wouldn't sell, would you? Well, that is all the union is doing—refusing to sell their labor.

First, what is the relevant similarity? The amount of money desired by someone is less than the amount being offered. The hidden generalization is that whenever too little is offered by a buyer to a seller for anything, it is appropriate to refuse to sell. But this generalization can be questioned on many grounds. Aren't there times when selling prices are too high? What are the consequences to society of high selling prices? Is management in the same situation as an individual consumer when it refuses to pay the seller's price?

This analogy is faulty because the underlying principle is flawed. When you encounter analogies, always evaluate the underlying principle. The analogy is not good proof; the principle may be.

Begging the Question

Sometimes a conclusion is supported by itself; only the words have been changed to fool the innocent! For example, to argue that dropping out of school is undesirable because it is bad is not to argue at all. The conclusion is "proven" by the conclusion (in different words). Such an argument *begs the question*, rather than answering it. Let's look at one that is a little less obvious.

> Programmed learning texts are clearly superior to traditional texts in learning effectiveness, since it is highly advantageous for learning to have materials presented in a step-by-step fashion.

Again, the reason supporting the conclusion restates the conclusion in different words. By definition, programmed learning is a step-by-step procedure. The writer is arguing that such a procedure is good because it is good.

Let's examine one more example.

> A comprehensive national health insurance plan is wasteful. Thus, passing such a bill would cause a great deal of harm. Since the bill would be so harmful, it is obviously a very wasteful bill.

How does the writer prove that passing the bill will be harmful? By claiming the bill is wasteful. How does he prove it is wasteful? By asserting the conclusion. Thus, the conclusion is used to support the reason which supports the conclusion. This is a special example of begging the question, commonly referred to as *circular reasoning*. The conclusion itself is used as proof for the assertion that is used to prove the conclusion. Thus, the conclusion has not been *proven;* it has been *assumed* in the proof.

Whenever something is *assumed* when it should be proven, begging the question has occurred. When you outline the structure of an argument, check the reasons to be sure that they do not simply repeat the conclusion in different words, and check to see that the conclusion is not used to prove the reasons. In case you are confused, let's illustrate with two examples, one argument that begs the question and one that does not.

> (1) To allow the press to keep their sources confidential is very advantageous to the country, because it increases the likelihood that individuals will report evidence against powerful people.

(2) To allow the press to keep their sources confidential is very advantageous to the country, because it is highly conducive to the interests of the larger community that private individuals should have the privilege of providing information to the press without being identified.

Paragraph (2) begs the question by basically repeating the conclusion. It fails to point out what the specific advantages are, and simply repeats that confidentiality of sources is socially useful.

Summary of Reasoning Errors

We have taken you through exercises that illustrate a number of ways in which reasoning may be erroneous. We have not listed all the ways, but we have given you a good start. To find errors in reasoning, keep in mind what kinds of reasons are good reasons—that is, the facts and the moral principles relevant to the issue. Reasoning should be rejected whenever erroneous assumptions are found. Reasoning should be rejected when it

> attacks a person or a person's background,
> presents a faulty dilemma,
> equivocates,
> oversimplifies,
> diverts attention from the issue,
> presents a faulty analogy,
> or begs the question.

Reasoning should be approached cautiously when it appeals to group-approved attitudes and to authority. You should always ask, Are there good reasons to consider such appeals as persuasive evidence? A precautionary note is in order here: Do not *automatically* reject reasoning that relies on analogy and appeals to authority or group-approved attitudes. Carefully evaluate such reasoning. For example, if most physicians in the country choose to take up jogging, that information is important to consider in deciding whether or not jogging is beneficial. Some authorities do possess valuable information. Also, analogy can be an extremely creative means by which to get us to see the relevant components of an issue.

Writing and Reasoning

When you write essays, you will necessarily engage in reasoning. Since you want your writing to be persuasive, it should be carefully reasoned. The last four chapters can be used as guidelines for your arguments. Awareness of possible errors that writers may commit provides you with warnings to heed. As you become more familiar with statistical and reasoning errors, your writing will improve. A checklist of possible errors will enable you to be your own censor. You can remove reasoning problems before your readers point them out to you.

Practice Exercises

◊ *Critical Question:* **Are there any errors in reasoning?**

Try to identify the reasoning errors in each of the three practice passages.

Passage 1

The following passage is a letter to the editor responding to a previous letter supporting the right of the Amish not to attend high school.

I would like to answer those misguided persons who have so eloquently defended the Amish people regarding their recent trouble with the law. I agree that pictures of people who have broken the law being marched off to jail are not pretty. But I would also like to remind your readers that freedom of religion gives no one the right to flout or break existing law.

If it can be proved that our present laws are bad with regard to the higher education of American citizens, let them be changed. But until that is done, let no "law-abiding," "God-fearing" Amish or anyone else disobey them. Laws are made for the good of all, whether or not these people, through ignorance or stupidity, know it.

Let's remember, too, that these same laws were recently defended by other loyal Americans at great cost, with but little support from the Amish and others of their ilk.

No Amish son died upon the battlefield. No Amish child must ask his mother why his soldier father never returned from the war.

People like these who refused to fight for their rights have little to complain about when we must force them to obey our laws, bought and delivered at the cost of loyal American lives.

I am quite sure they would be the first to impose their laws upon us should the shoe be on the other foot. If you question this, ask anyone who has lived in a community where their influence is strong. They are "law-abiding" people until they choose to act otherwise, as witness their disgraceful actions in recent weeks. By these they have again proved what basically poor excuses for Americans they are.

Obedience to the law
Freedom of choice

Passage 2

The following passage is a response to attacks on tax-deductible "three-martini" business lunches.

> You would indeed dry up jobs in the restaurant and entertainment business if you took away incentives for business lunch entertainment. More fundamental than that is the importance of creating business by using entertainment. Senator Long put it cogently; he said that business entertainment is to the corporate world what fertilizer is to agriculture; it makes for higher yields.[2]

Passage 3

Behind the Iron Curtain, the athletic system is basically the same as it is in America: the coach runs the athlete's entire life, in which every major decision is made by the coach. This process of decision making has developed the communist athletes into highly disciplined people, loyal to the state. Poets, scientists, and ballet dancers defect in hordes from the Eastern European countries, but communist athletes have chosen almost unanimously to remain in their home countries.

The American athlete, however, has been indoctrinated into the take-order complex of the carbon-copy totalitarian system. The inflexibility of the athletic system in America has turned us into a nation of hypocrites, preaching free will and choice while we produce millions of miniature fascists, primed to unleash the same system of law and order they were taught upon another generation of eager-to-please children.

From the first year of Little League to the last year of high school, the supreme status of the coach is impressed upon the athlete. Creativity is suppressed because of its subversive nature, and obedience is demanded. The budding athlete spends 6 years under the total control of the high school coach, preparing to spend another 4 years under the control of the college coach. If the athlete is highly successful, he will spend 10 additional years bending his knee to a professional coach.

If America is to remain a democracy, its major institutions must become democratic. It is impossible to expect athletes who someday will lead this country to be placed in an environment of oppression and to disregard that oppression. The oppression will surface at a later date. The

[2]Adapted from R. E. Kipling, "Conversation: The Three Martini Lunch," *Politics Today* (May/June 1978), 5.

greatest threat posed to democracy by sports is the graduation of sports figures into politics. Athletes carry their infection of fascism into the political world and turn government into a game, which it is most emphatically not. Nixon could ignore millions of protesters because they were players and he was the coach.

—————————————— **SAMPLE RESPONSES** ——————————————

Passage 1

We can structure this argument as follows:

CONCLUSION: *The Amish should have been jailed for refusing to send their children to school.*

REASONS: 1. *The law requires school attendance, and freedom of religion gives no one the right to break existing law.*
2. *These laws have been supported by loyal Americans but not by the Amish; people who have refused to fight for their rights have little to complain about when we force them to obey our laws.*
3. *They would be the first to impose their laws upon us should they be in the majority in our country. Their recent acts have proven what basically poor excuses for Americans they are.*

This is clearly a prescriptive argument, and no evidence is presented. The major issue is whether people should be jailed for following their religious beliefs when the beliefs conflict with the law. The writer's first reason is thus a value judgment which is directly relevant to the conclusion. If the value preference is accepted, the conclusion follows. Note that the other reasons given are basically direct attacks on the character of the Amish people, accompanied by appeals to the emotions. The arguments are basically *ad hominem*. The issue is not whether the Amish are good people or whether they have fought in our wars, but whether or not there are times when the law becomes secondary to religious beliefs. For example, if the Amish had "fought for our country" would this writer argue that they had the right to refuse to go to school? No. Thus, arguments 2 and 3 are invalid.

Passage 2

CONCLUSION: *We should maintain deductions for the three-martini lunch.*

REASONS: 1. *Taking away the deduction would dry up jobs in the restaurant and entertainment business.*
2. *Business entertainment is to the corporate world what fertilizer is to agriculture: it makes for a higher yield.*

First, we should again note that we have a prescriptive argument. Both reasons are generalizations, and reason 2 contains an analogy. Both reasons 1 and 2 note the advantage of the deductions—that they help business. Thus, if the reasons are true, and we accept the assumption that facilitating business profits is an important goal of our system of taxation, then the *reasoning* is valid. However, what about the truth of the reasons? Look at the analogy in reason 2. First we need to discover the relevant common characteristics. Both business entertainment and fertilizer may stimulate growth. But there are relevant differences that weaken the prospects for finding an illuminating principle in this analogy. We will mention a couple. Fertilizing the field and watching the corn grow do not provide the same personal pleasure as does having a $30 lunch at a gourmet restaurant. Also, there is a direct scientifically established causal link between applying fertilizer and seeing growth which does not exist between having a good meal and buying products. Thus, we should not accept the conclusion as true without better support than reason 2 provides.

Passage 3

CONCLUSION: *The American athletic system poses a threat to democracy.*

REASONS: *1. Our athletes are being indoctrinated into a fascist ideology. American coaches exert more oppressive control over the athlete than even communist coaches do. This control suppresses creativity and requires obedience.*

2. This ideology (the infection) is carried into the political world, turning government into a game. It is impossible to expect athletes placed in an environment of oppression not to reflect that same totalitarian characteristic when they become national leaders.

You should note several striking deficiencies in this rather complex argument. First, the reasons consist of a number of generalizations, but none of these are supported by any specific evidence. Thus, it is impossible to judge the truth of the reasons.

Second, the writer uses vague, emotionally loaded terms throughout the article. The words "cancer," "infection," "fascism," "oppression," and "carbon-copy totalitarian system" all tend to draw negative emotions from the reader. Until less emotional words are supplied and specific referents are given, it is impossible to judge either the truth of the reasons or the validity of the reasoning. For example, what specifically is meant by "an environment of oppression" or by "carry their infection of fascism into the political world"?

Third, the author of the passage is committing a form of the either-or fallacy. Only two choices are said to be available to us:

(a) Democracy, and a sports program that treats the coach as just one more member of the team, *or*

(b) Fascism, and our current sports program.

Isn't it likely that adjustments could be made in the existing relationship between coaches and their players (here we are assuming that the author's reasons are true) that would enable our democratic political institutions to survive? For example, every coach could be encouraged to remind his team repeatedly that the playing field is in many ways an inadequate model on which to base most important life decisions. The author of the passage does not consider any options beyond (a) and (b). Because of this sloppiness, we cannot accept the author's reasoning.

Passage 4 (Self-Examination)

Higher tuition suggests superior education. These schools called superior by books that rate the quality of colleges and universities are exactly those schools that cost the most to attend. Just as the quality of an automobile can be measured by its price tag, the worth of a particular school can be identified by its tuition.

Higher tuition permits higher salaries for professors. If professors are not kept happy by higher salaries, the quality of the teaching will suffer. The American Federation of Teachers points out that the contented faculty member is repeatedly the same one who is rated superior by her supervisors.

The point is that students have a vested interest in paying higher tuition. Those students who gripe about tuition are simply uninformed. We all know that you get what you pay for.

All inclusive
Study all tests.
Value assumption
excellence — material gain —

XII

What
Significant Information
Is Omitted?

You now know a number of good ways to identify weaknesses and strengths in arguments. The ability to spot ambiguities, misuse of evidence, and errors in reasoning is helpful in achieving this goal. We want to devote this chapter to an additional question you must ask in order to make reasonable personal decisions: What significant information is omitted? Sensitivity to missing information has been discussed briefly in several earlier chapters, but it is so important to critical reading that it deserves further emphasis.

Advertisers, teachers, politicians, authors, and parents all want to shape your decisions. It is a natural and highly predictable desire on their part. Typically, therefore, you will encounter only one side of a controversy when there may be dozens of possible conclusions and sets of arguments that would address the controversy. Those trying to persuade you will almost always present their position in the strongest possible light. So when you find what you believe to be strong reasons, it's wise to hesitate and to think about what the author may not have told you. These reasons may not be quite so impressive if you realize that their apparent strength is caused by the author's omission of significant information or of reasons that support different positions.

Interspersed throughout the chapter will be examples of reasoning that is not very convincing, not because of what is said but because of what is omitted. Look carefully at the examples and notice how in each case the failure to look for significant omitted information would have resulted in your making a premature decision.

◊   *Critical Question:*   **What significant information is omitted?**

The Certainty of Incomplete Reasoning

Incomplete reasoning is inevitable. A first explanation for this inevitability is the limitation imposed by time and space. Arguments are incomplete because writers do not have forever to organize them, nor do they have unlimited space in which to present their reasons. Second, the attention span of most of us is very limited; we get bored when messages are too long. Thus, writers often feel a need to get their messages across quickly. Advertising reflects both these factors. The time allotted for presenting the advertising message is short, and the message must both attract and retain your attention. Advertisers consequently engage in many annoying omissions.

For example, a well-known deodorant commercial compares the effectiveness of the advertised brand's roll-on with that for spray versions of several other deodorants. Not surprisingly, the roll-on "lasts longer." Should we then conclude that the advertised brand of roll-on deodorant is superior to others? Wait just a minute! What the advertisement neglects to include is any information about the relative effectiveness of roll-ons and sprays in general. A relevant piece of omitted information would be such comparative data. If roll-ons are always more effective than spray deodorants, then the advertisement is persuading us to act in a manner not necessarily consistent with our best interests. Perhaps any roll-on (not necessarily the advertised brand) would last longer than any spray deodorant. The advertiser omitted significant data that you would need if you were to buy wisely.

Another type of missing information is at least as important. Even had there not been missing data in the advertisement, you would still want to consider other possible advantages or disadvantages of different deodorants. The advertiser does not mention price. Why? We can only guess, but he must think you are more interested in the product's effectiveness than in its price. If your values are different, you may not be highly impressed by the longer lasting quality of the advertised deodorant.

A third reason for the inevitability of missing information is that the knowledge possessed by the person making the argument will always be incomplete. For example, no one can know *everything* about the assassination of John F. Kennedy. Consequently, anyone claiming to know who killed Kennedy must be omitting information that would be helpful to you if you were carefully trying to make up your mind about the identity of the assassin. Similarly, when over half the doctors sampled in a survey of attitudes toward national health insurance fail to complete the questionnaire, it is impossible to know whether or not they differ in significant ways from the doctors who do complete the survey. Yet this is a very important piece of information.

A fourth reason why information may be omitted is because of an outright attempt to deceive. Advertisers *know* they are omitting key bits of information. If they were to describe all the chemicals or cheap component parts that go into their products, you would be less likely to buy them. Experts in every field consciously omit information when open disclosure would weaken the persuasive effect of their advice. Such omissions are particularly tempting if those trying to advise you see you as a "sponge."

A final important reason why omitted information is so prevalent is that the values, beliefs, and attitudes of those trying to advise or persuade you are frequently different from yours. You can expect, therefore, that their reasoning will be guided by different assumptions than those you would have brought to the same question. A particular perspective is like a pair of blinders on a horse. The blinders improve the tendency of the horse to focus on what is directly in front of him. Yet, an individual's perspective, like blinders on a horse, prevents her from noting certain information that would be important to those who reason from a different frame of reference. Unless your perspective is identical to that of the person trying to persuade you, important omissions of information are to be expected.

Let's review. Omitted information is inevitable. There are at least five reasons for the prevalence of omitted information:

1. Time and space limitations
2. Limited attention span
3. Inadequacies in human knowledge
4. Deception
5. Different perspectives

Do you now see the danger of the sponge model even more clearly? You must actively question expertise and advice if you are to avoid forming opinions based on unnecessarily limited information.

Questions that Identify Omitted Information

If you are now convinced that reasoning will necessarily be incomplete, you may ask, What am I supposed to do? Well, initially you have to remind yourself again and again that regardless of how attractive the reasons supporting a particular decision or opinion may be at first glance, it's necessary to take another look in search of omitted information. How do you search, and what can you expect to find? You ask questions to help decide what additional information you need, and then ask questions designed to reveal that information.

Isn't it silly to ask questions of a writer who cannot answer? Not at all! Although the writer won't answer your questions, asking them has positive results. First, you may be able to supply the missing information because of what you already know. Second, searching for omitted information in written persuasion gives you good practice for when you *are* able to search for omitted information face-to-face with a teacher or anyone else who is trying to persuade you orally. Even more importantly, searching for omitted information prevents you from making up your mind too soon.

By asking such questions of written material, you are reminding yourself that the information provided is incomplete. Whatever conclusion you reach on the basis of incomplete information will necessarily be tentative. You cannot be sure about the accuracy of your opinion as long as important information is missing.

The questions you can use to find omitted information are similar to those you have encountered in earlier chapters. Asking critical questions about ambiguity, the use of evidence, and the quality of assumptions usually highlights omitted information.

Important types of missing information include the following:

1. Key definitions
2. Alternative techniques for gathering or organizing the evidence
3. Omitted effects of what is advocated and of what is opposed
4. Missing graphs or data

Take a look at some arguments that have omitted some or all of the types of information listed. Watch how each of the omissions might cause you to form a faulty conclusion. Only by asking that omitted information be supplied in each case could you avoid this danger.

Initially, let's look at an advertising claim. Several cereals are advertised as providing "part of a balanced breakfast." What is meant by the word *part* here? Wouldn't you like to know how large this part is, relative to that in other cereals? Of course, unless you do not mind wasting money. Thus, the advertiser has omitted a key definition. Remember that the goal of the seller is different from yours. The cereal firm wants a sale; you want taste, economy, and nutrition. Consequently, you should expect the advertisement to omit certain information that is crucial to your particular purpose if that omission enlarges sales. One important additional bit of omitted information is the effect on your health of consuming the large amounts of sugar contained in many sugar-coated cereals, an effect that advertisers would prefer not to mention.

Let's now take a look at a more complicated example. Read the following excerpt and ask yourself what has been omitted.

A young person once had a pretty sure prospect of getting a good job and high salary by going to college. Now that certainty is no longer there.

There was a big increase in the number of young people graduating from colleges and universities in the 70s. The demand for college graduates has simply not increased at that pace. One of the sectors where college graduates have traditionally been employed has been in teaching; however, the demand for teachers has fallen. The federal bureaucracy, a major employer of college graduates, has not been expanding in the last several years.

The earnings gap between high school and college graduates has narrowed significantly. Bureau of the Census data indicate that, for the average college graduate aged 25 and over, the advantage declined from about 53 percent in 1969 to 35 or 36 percent in 1977.[1]

What important information was omitted? Did you ask questions that would identify any of the four types of omitted information that we described for you? Let us help you. How did the economist measure what it meant for a college degree to be worth the price? Did his definition of what a college degree is worth reflect a value assumption with which you agree? Did the author of the excerpt examine the most important effects to you of a college education? What useful data are missing? For example, wouldn't it be helpful to know how satisfied college graduates are with their jobs? Obviously, the writer gave you only a partial picture of the value of a college degree. Unless you complete the picture, your decision about whether to go to or continue in college will be very uninformed.

Omitted Information that Remains Missing

Just because you are able to request important missing information does not guarantee a satisfactory response. It is quite possible that your probing questions cannot be answered. Do not despair! You did your part. You requested information which you needed to make up your mind; you must now decide whether it is possible to arrive at a conclusion without the missing information. We warned you earlier that reasoning is always incomplete. Therefore, to claim automatically that you cannot make a decision as long as information is missing would prevent you from ever forming any opinions. The information you need to be perfectly certain that you are right will never be available.

Practice Exercises

◊   *Critical Question:*   **What significant information is omitted?**

In each of the following examples, there is important missing information. Make a list of questions you would ask the person who wrote each passage. Explain in each case why the information you are seeking is important to you as you try to decide the worth of the reasoning.

[1]Adapted from R. Freeman, "Does It Pay to Go to College?," *U.S. News & World Report* (24 January 1977), 59–60.

Passage 1

The *Wall Street Journal* charged that Holiday Inns had the worst fire record of the ten major U.S. hotel-motel chains in the last decade, a toll of 29 deaths and 216 injuries in 26 serious fires. The newspaper said that, among the major hotel companies, Holiday Inns operated 29 percent of all the rooms, but that it had experienced 39 percent of the serious fires, 55 percent of the deaths, 37 percent of the injuries, and 39 percent of the damage. The *Journal* charged that this poor record was due, in part, to some design features of the chain's low-rise motels.

Passage 2

What all the evidence seems to suggest is that some violence portrayed on television could make some TV watchers violent. But consider how many people are killed by tranquilizers. Does that mean we should eliminate them? A generation was raised on westerns and detective shows. If critics are right about the brutalizing effects of television on youth, why didn't young people want to rush off to Vietnam to vent their aggressions? Instead, they did a lot to protest that war and bring it to a stop.

Passage 3

The volunteer service is a failure. The volunteer force could not possibly work in a war. What we have now is a peacetime volunteer force, with the inevitability that if we had a war—even a limited war—we'd have to go back to the draft.

The Army is about 100,000 recruits short in its individual Ready Reserve Forces, and projections indicate that it will be about 500,000 short in the early 1990s. The Army itself is experiencing recruiting difficulties; it is about 9 percent under their quota so far in fiscal year '84.

———————————— SAMPLE RESPONSES ————————————

Passage 1

CONCLUSION: *Holiday Inns are greater fire risks than are other hotel-motel chains.*

REASON: *Evidence shows that Holiday Inns experience fires resulting in deaths and injuries disproportionate to the number of rooms they operate.*

If you were the president of Holiday Inns, you might argue that the full picture has not been presented. What relevant information is omitted?

What is Holiday Inns' occupancy rate? Maybe more of their rooms tend to be occupied, increasing the likelihood of fires. How many serious fires occurred? If there were only a few, the percentages reported may not be very meaningful. Do most fires occur in chain hotels? Perhaps independent hotels have a higher rate of fires.

Passage 2

Order free

CONCLUSION: *We should not place additional restrictions on television violence.*

REASONS: 1. *It does not make sense to eliminate something like television violence just because it harms a few people. We have not eliminated tranquilizers, even though they harm some people.*
   2. *The same young people who watched so much violence on television actively resisted the war in Vietnam. Their actions demonstrate that watching television violence does not make one more violent.*

This passage omits important data as well as significant disadvantages of failing to regulate the amount of television violence. For instance, there were many young people who supported the war in Vietnam. How can we know the effects of television violence on attitudes toward war unless we have comparative data on the attitudes of frequent and infrequent television viewers? The author of the passage also omits any reference to the positive correlation shown in many studies between observing violence on television and engaging in violent crimes. What specifically is meant by *some* effect on *some* people? If the effect is mass murders, we would be very concerned.

Passage 3

CONCLUSION: *The volunteer army is a failure.*

REASONS: 1. *Too few recruits have been attracted to the volunteer service. We could never fight a war with such a service because we cannot attract enough people even during peacetime.*
   2. *The current ready reserves are hundreds of thousands short.*

As with many arguments, this one does not include any evidence that would weaken its reasoning. Does any evidence exist that would enable us to conclude that the volunteer army is a success? For example, does the composition of the current army provide a more representative cross-section of our population than that prevalent under the draft?

For the first reason to be convincing, we would need to know what the effect of patriotism would be on enlistments during a war. Is it fair to project a shortage of manpower during peace into a prospective period of war (assuming that war has more public support than did the Vietnam War)?

Before responding to the second reason, we would need to know how "short" is determined. Who makes the quotas and on what basis? What are the financial costs of meeting these quotas? What are the advantages of maintaining a small reserve?

Passage 4 (Self-Examination)

The great danger of television is that it requires so little mental effort to watch. Television gives us thousands of images of war, leisure, marriage, police, adolescence, and death, offering its viewers a prepackaged reality that we are asked to absorb rather than evaluate. As a result, we don't have to strive to develop our own understandings of these events or groups. Our brains can relax while the television implants images in them.

Think of the damage television does to our educational system. Teachers increasingly tell us that students cannot concentrate for an extended period. A comparison of college textbooks from 20 years ago with those published now shows an increased use of pictures and simplistic vocabulary and a dramatic decline in the number of words. Distinctions and nuances are ignored in a desperate effort to attract the attention of readers reared on television images. But many of our most valuable ideas are complex. Will future citizens quickly discount these insights as "boring" simply because they require extended concentration to appreciate?

Contrast the mental process that accompanies reading with that which occurs during television viewing. The reader controls the pace of image formation and development. She can reflect on a sentence and even return to earlier sentences in search of a meaning that escaped her the first time through. She may choose to reflect on the extent to which the passage reminds her of her own experiences or enriches her hopes. Television gives little time for such creative use of imagination. The pace continues without pauses—except for the next commercial.

XIII

What Alternative Conclusions Are Consistent with the Strong Reasons?

By this stage you should have acquired the filters required to distinguish stronger reasons from weaker ones. Strong reasons are those you are least able to criticize. After you have identified the stronger reasons, there is one additional step that will be useful to you in preparing for a personal decision concerning the controversy in question. This final step in the evaluation process consists of identifying the various inferences that can be based on the strong reasons.

Very rarely will you have a situation in which only one conclusion can be reasonably inferred from the strong reasons. Consequently, you must make sure that the conclusion you eventually adopt is the most reasonable and the most consistent with your value preferences. If you are still undecided about which inference is best after you have identified those that can be drawn from the strong reasons, your conclusion will be especially tentative. The recognition that the strong reasons could provide support for conclusions different from yours should heighten your interest in any further tests or studies that would help identify the best conclusion.

◊   *Critical Question:* **What alternative conclusions are consistent with the strong reasons?**

Assumptions and Alternative Conclusions

Neither a set of facts attempting to support a generalization nor a group of strong reasons supporting a prescriptive conclusion can be interpreted in only one way. Facts and reasons do not generally speak for themselves in an obvious way. As we have seen many times, conclusions are reached only after someone makes certain interpretations or assumptions concerning the meaning of the reasons and evidence.

If you make a different assumption concerning the meaning of the reasons and evidence, you will reach different conclusions. Since we all possess different levels of perceptual precision, frames of reference, and prior knowledge in general, we repeatedly disagree about which conclusions are preferable. We form different conclusions from strong reasons because our diverse backgrounds and goals cause us to be attracted to different assumptions when we decide to link reasons to conclusions.

Sometimes a writer will mention alternative conclusions that can be reached on the basis of the reasons he has presented. However, it will often be necessary for *you* to generate possible alternative inferences. To perform this creative task, try to imagine what different assumptions might enable someone to jump from the strong reasons you have identified to another inference. Remember, *many* possible inferences can be made on the basis of most sets of strong reasons. The next section is designed to help you recognize the multiplicity of possible conclusions.

Two Sides or Many?

There are very few important questions that can be answered with a simple yes or an absolute no. Once an issue is addressed and you have carefully analyzed the reasoning, there are probably still several conclusions that might be reasonable. Many of the previous questions you have been urged to ask are the same questions that will help you to search for alternative inferences or conclusions. Before we look at several arguments in which alternative inferences are possible, let's make sure that you appreciate the large number of conclusions that are possible with respect to most important controversies. Here are three contemporary questions.

1. Do IQ tests measure intelligence?
2. Is the president's energy package desirable?
3. Should judges be elected or appointed?

At first glance, these questions and many like them seem to call for yes or no answers. However, a qualified maybe is often the best answer. The advantage of maybe as an answer is that it forces you to admit that you do not yet know enough to make a definitive answer. But at the same time that you are avoiding a definite answer, you have formed a tentative decision or opinion that calls for commitment and eventual action. Once you recognize that you can never be certain how to answer complex questions, you can better accept the necessity of making decisions even when you know you are missing critical information or understanding. It's wise to seek additional information that would improve the support for your opinions, but at some point you must stop searching and make a decision, even when the most forceful answer you are willing to defend is a "yes, but . . ."

Glance back at the three questions that preceded the last paragraph. Ask yourself what conclusions would be possible in response to each question. Naturally, a yes or a no answer would be two possible conclusions. Are there others? Yes, many! Let's look at just a few of the possible answers to the first of these questions.

Do IQ tests measure intelligence?

1. Yes, to the extent that intelligence means sequential reasoning.
2. Yes, when they are given to children of the same sociocultural background.
3. Yes, if they are used only for elementary school children.
4. Yes, when the IQ scores are highly correlated with measures of motivation.
5. Yes, but only in terms of the type of intelligence that is useful in schools.
6. No, if you define intelligence as that factor which leads to later success in one's chosen field.
7. No, if they fail to include data gathered orally.

Notice that in each case we added a condition that is necessary before the alternative inference can be justified. In the absence of any data or definitions, any of these seven conclusions could be the most reasonable. We would hope to be better able to choose from among these inferences after analyzing the strong arguments. These seven are just a few of the conclusions possible for the first question. Thus, there may be many possible answers to a question, not just two.

Just for practice, try to suggest five possible conclusions for the third question: Should judges be elected or appointed?

Perhaps this conclusion occurred to you: *Elected, if it can be demonstrated that most of those who would vote understand the tasks of a judge well enough to make a choice consistent with efficient justice.* Or maybe you thought of this one: *Appointed, in those states where the voter turnout in state legislative races has averaged more than 50 percent in the last 10 years?* But probably neither of these appears on your list. Why are we so sure? Because there are an enormous number of possible conclusions for this question. It would be an unlikely coincidence if you had chosen either of these two from the huge list of possible conclusions. This great number of answers is what we want you to grasp. Knowledge of the possibility of multiple conclusions will prevent you from leaping to one prematurely.

Searching for Alternative Conclusions

This section contains two arguments that point out alternative inferences that could be created from the reasons in each argument. The intention is to give you some models to use when you search for alternative inferences. In each case, we will give you the structure of the argument before we suggest alternative conclusions. One clue to help you in your search is the following: Study the strong reasons without looking at the conclusion, and try to identify as many inferences as possible that would follow from the reasons.

CONCLUSION: *Those who refuse to serve in wars should not be pardoned.*

REASONS: 1. *They are not sorry for what they did.*
2. *A pardon would increase the likelihood that many would refuse to fight in future wars.*
3. *Our already embattled military would feel even more under attack by this rejection of their past contributions.*

Looking at the first reason, we might arrive at entirely different conclusions depending on the definition of *pardon*. The ambiguity in the word permits many alternative conclusions. Each definition might enable us to reach a different conclusion of the following form: *If the writer defines "pardon" as—*——, *then my position would be that*——.
For example, if the writer defines pardon as removing all potential legal penalties in return for which the draft resister must pay no social penalties, then my position would be. . . .

Another way to generate alternative inferences would be by a careful examination of the three reasons as a group. It is possible to accept the truth of all three reasons and still to arrive at several different conclusions. For example: *Since our country does not value international harmony to the extent it should, a pardon is desirable as a stimulus for debate that might reorient our nation's foreign policy.*

CONCLUSION: *Congress should not decriminalize marijuana.*

REASONS: 1. *A group of British scientists have shown that smoking marijuana may cause serious brain damage.*
2. *Marijuana smokers risk decreasing their fertility.*
3. *Marijuana smokers often become heroin users.*

What alternative conclusions are possible? One would be to decriminalize marijuana in one locale and observe the impact before making a national rule. Alternatively, Congress could sponsor research designed to develop a substance that would produce effects similar to those produced by marijuana without the possible side effects. Another possibility, based on a strong devotion to the value of individual responsibility, would be to permit pot to be sold in stores along with other possibly hazardous materials, the assumption being that those who may misuse the drug have a right to do so. Observe that all three of these conclusions are possible even if we accept the truth of the three reasons. Thus, the same reasons frequently can be used to support several different conclusions.

Productivity of If-Clauses

If you went back over all the alternative inferences discussed in this chapter, you would notice that each optional conclusion is possible because we are missing certain information, definitions, assumptions, or the frame of reference of the person analyzing the reasons. Consequently, we can create alternative inferences by the judicious use of *if-clauses*. In an if-clause, we state a condition which we are assuming in order to enable us to reach a particular inference. Notice that the use of if-clauses permits us to arrive at a conclusion without pretending that we know more than we actually do about a particular controversy.

When you use if-clauses to precede conclusions, you are pointing out that your inference is based on particular claims or assumptions about which you are uncertain. To see what we mean, look at some sample conditional statements that might precede inferences.

1. If she is referring to freedom of religion when she speaks of the loss of our basic freedom, then . . .
2. If the birth rate continues to rise over the next 5 years, then . . .
3. If we look at his sales record from the FDA's perspective, then . . .

These if-clauses present you with alternative inferences that you may wish to assess before making up your mind about the controversy, and broaden the list of possible conclusions from which you can choose your opinion.

Practice Exercises

◊   *Critical Question:* **What alternative conclusions are consistent with the strong reasons?**

For each of the following arguments, identify three different alternative conclusions that could be drawn from the reasons.

Passage 1

A recent survey found that more than half of the $50 billion spent annually on automobile repairs was wasted. The survey covered 62 garages in seven cities. The survey found that many unnecessary services were performed and that the work was often of poor quality. In addition, only half the garages visited were judged "fair" in terms of the prices they charged.

What can be done to reduce this waste? A few well-publicized prosecutions might do wonders. Those who take advantage of consumer ignorance are the worst variety of thief. Consumers should make a special effort to see that such garages go broke by not taking sick automobiles to these rip-off artists.

Passage 2

The use of racial quotas for either college admission or employment is wrong. Quotas represent an immoral technique for achieving important objectives. It makes little sense to say that we should create a fair world by unfair means. Equality is desirable, but not at any cost.

In addition, quotas are actually harmful for those whom they are intended to help. It is cruel to place a person in a position where she will be underqualified, since such a person is certain to feel her inadequacy. Many people who receive their positions as a result of quotas will drop out, feeling more unhappy than they felt before the quota was established.

Passage 3

In the future, nuclear power will simply be so expensive that it will not be feasible. Many of the utilities that sponsored the expansion of nuclear facilities are now either cancelling or postponing their plans for new plants. In addition, nuclear power is associated with unacceptable health and safety risks. If a major nuclear disaster were to occur, who knows the genetic and ecological damage that would result? We cannot base our energy hopes on such a dangerous source.

—————————————— Sample Responses ——————————————

Passage 1

CONCLUSION: *Those responsible for automobile repair rip-offs should be prosecuted for fraud.*

REASONS: 1. *More than half the annual expenditure on automobile repairs is wasted.*

2. *Well-publicized prosecutions of the guilty repair shops will serve as a deterrent and inform consumers as to which garages to avoid.*

The author's inference is but one of several that are consistent with the reasons. These include the following:

If the repairs are faulty because of undertrained mechanics, a better solution to the problem would be the licensing of mechanics.

If we assume that mechanics are urged to check automobiles not just for current problems but for impending ones as well, it's possible that the survey data was focusing on a narrow definition of "waste." Perhaps one could thus infer that mechanics should generally be praised for their long-range care of our automobiles.

The automobile is such a complicated mechanism that it's unrealistic to expect repair records any better than those reported in the survey.

Passage 2

CONCLUSION: *Racial quotas in colleges and jobs are wrong.*

REASONS: 1. *Racial quotas are immoral and illegal because they violate our standards of equality.*

2. *Quotas harm those who receive jobs or positions, because they are embarrassed and hurt when they fail.*

In this passage there is again a woeful lack of evidence. For purposes of this exercise, however, we will simply assume the truth of these reasons. From the reasons, we could reach the following conclusions:

We should encourage affirmative action policies as an alternative to quotas.

Equality of result is more important than equality as the author is defining it. Thus, we should encourage quotas as a means of providing equality of result, especially after we have insured that those who benefit from quotas can, through proper training, succeed at least as often as their white counterparts.

We should enlarge our efforts to teach black history so that more people realize that we need to develop a new standard of equality. With this revised standard, we could create an environment in which quotas would lead to a higher form of equality rather than to failure.

Passage 3

CONCLUSION: *Nuclear energy should not be a major energy source.*

REASONS: 1. *It is too costly.*
2. *It is dangerous to our health and safety.*

These two reasons are consistent with several conflicting inferences.

Nuclear energy development should be encouraged, because even with its disadvantages it is the energy source with the fewest risks.

We should spend more money on the newer nuclear fusion research.

If Congress grants the requested funds, nuclear energy can be made relatively cheap and safe in the long run.

Passage 4 (Self-Examination): Complex Passage

The Case Against Helping the Poor[1]

Garret Hardin

Environmentalists use the metaphor of the earth as a "spaceship" in trying to persuade countries, industries, and people to stop wasting and polluting our natural resources. Since we all share life on this planet, they argue, no single person or institution has the right to destroy, waste, or use more than a fair share of its resources.

But does everyone on earth have an equal right to an equal share of its resources? The spaceship metaphor can be dangerous when used by misguided idealists to justify suicidal policies for sharing our resources through uncontrolled immigration and foreign aid. In their enthusiastic but unrealistic generosity, they confuse the ethics of a spaceship with those of a lifeboat.

A true spaceship would have to be under the control of a captain, since no ship could possibly survive if its course were determined by committee. Spaceship Earth certainly has no captain; the United Nations is merely a toothless tiger, with little power to enforce any policy upon its bickering members.

If we divide the world crudely into rich nations and poor nations, two-thirds of them are desperately poor, and only one-third comparatively rich, with the United States the wealthiest of all. Metaphorically each rich nation can be seen as a lifeboat full of comparatively rich people. In the ocean outside each lifeboat swim the poor of the world, who would like to get in, or at least to share some of the wealth. What should the lifeboat passengers do?

First, we must recognize the limited capacity of any lifeboat. For example, a nation's land has a limited capacity to support a population and as the current energy crisis has shown us, in some ways we have already exceeded the carrying capacity of our land.

Adrift in a Moral Sea. So here we sit, say, 50 people in our lifeboat. To be generous, let us assume it has room for 10 more, making a total capacity of 60. Suppose the 50 of us in the lifeboat see 100 others swimming in the water outside, begging for admission to our boat or for handouts. We have several options: We may be tempted to try to live by the Christian ideal of being "our brother's keeper," or by the Marxist ideal of "to each according to his needs." Since the needs of all in the water are the same, and since they can all be seen as "our brothers," we could take them all into our boat, making a total of 150 in a boat designed for 60. The boat swamps, everyone drowns. Complete justice, complete catastrophe.

Since the boat has an unused excess capacity of 10 more passengers, we could admit just 10 more to it. But which 10 do we let in? How do we choose? Do we pick the best 10, the neediest 10, "first come, first served"? And what do we say to the 90 we exclude? If we do let an extra 10 into our lifeboat, we will have lost our "safety factor," an engineering principle of critical importance. For example, if we don't leave room for excess capacity as a safety factor in our country's agriculture, a new plant disease or a bad change in the weather could have disastrous consequences.

Suppose we decide to preserve our small safety factor and admit no more to the lifeboat. Our survival is then possible, although we shall have to be constantly on guard against boarding parties.

While this last solution clearly offers the only means of our survival, it is morally abhorrent to many people. Some say they feel guilty about their good luck. My reply is simple. "Get out and yield your place to others." This may solve the problem of the guilt-ridden person's conscience, but it does not change the ethics of the lifeboat. The needy person to whom the guilt-ridden person yields his place will not himself feel guilty about his good luck. If he did, he would not climb aboard. The net result of conscience-stricken people giving up their unjustly held seats is the elimination of that sort of conscience from the lifeboat.

This is the basic metaphor within which we must work out our solutions. Let us now enrich the image, step by step, with substantive additions from the real world, a world that must solve real and pressing problems of overpopulation and hunger.

The harsh ethics of the lifeboat become even harsher when we consider the reproductive differences between the rich nations and the poor nations. The people inside the lifeboat are doubling in numbers every 87 years; those swimming around outside are doubling, on the average, every 35 years, more than twice as fast as the rich. And since the world's resources are dwindling, the difference in prosperity between the rich and the poor can only increase.

As of 1973, the U.S. had a population of 210 million people, who were increasing by 0.8 percent per year. Outside our lifeboat, let us imagine another 210 million people (say the combined populations of Colombia, Ecuador, Venezuela, Morocco, Pakistan, Thailand, and the Philippines), who are increasing at a rate of 3.3 percent per year. Put differently, the doubling time for this aggregate population is 21 years, compared to 87 years for the U.S.

Multiplying the Rich and the Poor. Now suppose the U.S. agreed to pool its resources with those seven countries, with everyone receiving an equal share. Initially the ratio of Americans to non-Americans in this model would be one-to-one. But consider what the ratio would be after 87 years, by which time the Americans would have doubled to a population of 420 million. By then, doubling every 21 years, the other group would have swollen to 354 billion. Each American would have to share the available resources with more than eight people.

But, one could argue, this discussion assumes that current population trends will continue, and they may not. Quite so. Most likely the rate of population increase will decline much faster in the U.S. than it will in the other countries, and there does not seem to be much we can do about it. In sharing with "each according to his needs," we must recognize that needs are determined by population size, which is determined by the rate of reproduction, which at present is regarded as a sovereign right of every nation, poor or not. This being so, the philanthropic load created by the sharing ethic of the spaceship can only increase.

The Tragedy of the Commons. The fundamental error of spaceship ethics, and the sharing it requires, is that it leads to what I call "the tragedy of the commons." Under a system of private property, the men who own property recognize their responsibility to care for it, for if they don't they will eventually suffer. A farmer, for instance, will allow no more cattle in a pasture than its carrying capacity justifies. If he overloads it, erosion sets in, weeds take over, and he loses the use of the pasture.

If a pasture becomes a commons open to all, the right of each to use it may not be matched by a corresponding responsibility to protect it. Asking everyone to use it with discretion will hardly do, for the considerate herdsman who refrains from overloading the commons suffers more than a selfish one who says his needs are greater. If everyone would restrain himself, all would be well; but it takes only one less than everyone to ruin a system of voluntary restraint. In a crowded world of less than perfect human beings, mutual ruin is inevitable if there are no controls. This is the tragedy of the commons.

One of the major tasks of education today should be the creation of such an acute awareness of the dangers of the commons that people will recognize its many varieties. For example, the air and water have become polluted because they are treated as commons. Further growth in the population or per-capita conversion of natural resources into pollutants will only make the problem worse. The same holds true for the fish of the oceans. Fishing fleets have nearly disappeared in many parts of the world; technological improvements in the art of fishing are hastening the day of complete ruin. Only the replacement of the system of the commons with a responsible system of control will save the land, air, water, and oceanic fisheries.

The World Food Bank. In recent years there has been a push to create a new commons called a World Food Bank, an international depository of food reserves to which nations would contribute according to their abilities and from which they would draw according to their needs. This humanitarian proposal has received support from many liberal international groups, and from such prominent citizens as Margaret Mead, U.N. Secretary General Kurt Waldheim, and Senators Edward Kennedy and George McGovern.

A world food bank appeals powerfully to our humanitarian impulses. But before we rush ahead with such a plan, let us recognize where the greatest political push comes from, lest we be disillusioned later. Our experience with the "Food for Peace Program," or Public Law 480, gives us the answer. This program moved billions of dollars worth of U.S. surplus grain to food-short, population-long countries during the past two decades. But when P.L. 480 first became law, a headline in the business magazine *Forbes* revealed the real power behind it. "Feeding the World's Hungry Millions: How It Will Mean Billions for U.S. Business."

And indeed it did. In the years 1960 to 1970, U.S. taxpayers spent a total of $7.9 billion on the Food for Peace program. Between 1948 and 1970, they also paid an additional $50 billion for other economic-aid programs, some of which went for food and food-producing machinery and technology. Though all U.S. taxpayers were forced to contribute to the cost of P.L. 480, certain special interest groups gained handsomely under the program. Farmers did not have to contribute the grain; the government, or rather the taxpayers, bought it from them at full market prices. The increased demand raised prices of farm products generally. The manufacturers of farm machinery, fertilizers and pesticides benefited by the farmers' extra efforts to grow more food. Grain elevators profited from storing the surplus until it could be shipped. Railroads made money hauling it to ports, and shipping lines profited from carrying it overseas. The implementation of P.L. 480 required the creation of a vast government bureaucracy, which then acquired its own vested interest in continuing the program regardless of its merits.

Extracting Dollars. Those who proposed and defended the Food for Peace program in public rarely mentioned its importance to any of these special interests. The public emphasis was always on its humanitarian effects. The combination of silent selfish interests and highly vocal humanitarian apologists made a powerful and succesful lobby for extracting money from taxpayers. We can expect the same lobby to push now for the creation of a World Food Bank.

However great the potential benefit to selfish interests, it should not be a decisive argument against a truly humanitarian program. We must ask if such a program would actually do more good than harm, not only momentarily but also in the long run. Those who propose the food bank usually refer to a current "emergency" or "crisis" in terms of world food supply. But what is an emergency? Although they may be infrequent and sudden, everyone knows that emergencies will occur from time to time. A well-run family, company, organization, or country prepares for the likelihood of accidents and emergencies. It expects them, it budgets for them, it saves for them.

Learning the Hard Way. What happens if some organizations or countries budget for accidents and others do not? If each country is solely responsible for its own well-being, poorly managed ones will suffer. But they can learn from experience. They may mend their ways, and learn to budget for infrequent but certain emergencies. For example, the weather varies from year to year, and periodic crop failures are certain. A wise and competent government saves out of the production of the good years in anticipation of bad years to come. Joseph taught this policy to Pharaoh in Egypt more than 2,000 years ago. Yet the great majority of the governments in the world today do not follow such a policy. They lack either the wisdom or the competence, or both. Should those nations that do manage to put something aside be forced to come to the rescue each time an emergency occurs among the poor nations?

"But is isn't their fault!" Some kindhearted liberals argue. "How can we blame the poor people who are caught in an emergency? Why must they suffer for the sins of their governments?" The concept of blame is simply not relevant here. the real question is, what are the operational consequences of establishing a food bank? If it is open to every country every time a need develops, slovenly rulers will not be motivated to take Joseph's advice. Someone will always come to their aid. Some countries will deposit food in the world food bank, and others will withdraw it. There will be almost no overlap. As a result of such solutions to food shortage emergencies, the poor countries will not learn to mend their ways, and will suffer progressively greater emergencies as their populations grow.

Population Control the Crude Way. On the average, poor countries undergo a 2.5 percent increase in population each year; rich countries, about 0.8 percent. Only rich countries have anything in the way of food reserves set aside, and even they do not have as much as they should. Poor countries have none. If poor countries received no food from the outside, the rate of their population growth would be periodically checked by crop failures and famines. But if they can always draw on a world food bank in time of need, their population can continue to grow unchecked, and so will their "need" for aid. In the short run, a world food bank may diminish that need, but in the long run it actually increases the need without limit.

Without some system of worldwide food sharing, the proportion of people in the rich and poor nations might eventually stabilize. The overpopulated poor countries would decrease in numbers, while the rich countries that had room for more people would increase. But with a well-meaning system of sharing, such as a world food bank, the growth differential between the rich and the poor countries will not only persist, it will increase. Because of the higher rate of population growth in the poor countries of the world, 88 percent of today's children are born poor, and only 12 percent rich. Year by year the ratio becomes worse, as the fast-reproducing poor outnumber the slow-reproducing rich.

A world food bank is thus a commons in disguise. People will have more motivation to draw from it than to add to any common store. The less provident and less able will multiply at the expense of the abler and more provident, bringing eventual ruin upon all who share in the commons. Besides, any system of "sharing" that amounts to foreign aid from the rich nations to the poor nations will carry the taint of charity, which will contribute little to the world peace so devoutly desired by those who support the idea of a world food bank.

As past U.S. foreign-aid programs have amply and depressingly demonstrated, international charity frequently inspires mistrust and antagonism rather than gratitude on the part of the recipient nation.

Pure Justice vs. Reality. Clearly, the concept of pure justice produces an infinite regression to absurdity. Centuries ago, wise men invented statutes of limitations to justify the rejection of such pure justice, in the interest of preventing continual disorder. The law zealously defends property right, but only relatively recent property rights. Drawing a line after an arbitrary time has elapsed may be unjust, but the alternatives are worse.

We are all the descendants of thieves, and the world's resources are inequitably distributed. But we must begin the journey to tomorrow from the point where we are today. We cannot remake the past. We cannot safely divide the wealth equitably among all peoples so long as people reproduce at different rates. To do so would guarantee that our grandchildren, and everyone else's grandchildren, would have only a ruined world to inhabit.

To be generous with one's own possessions is quite different from being generous with those of posterity. We should call this point to the attention of those who, from a commendable love of justice and equality, would institute a system of the commons, either in the form of a world food bank, or of unrestricted immigration. We must convince them if we wish to save at least some parts of the world from environmental ruin.

Without a true world government to control reproduction and the use of available resources, the sharing ethic of the spaceship is impossible. For the foreseeable future, our survival demands that we govern our actions by the ethics of a lifeboat, harsh though they may be. Posterity will be satisfied with nothing less.

XIV

What Are Your
Value Preferences
in this Controversy?

This chapter shifts the focus from issues of truth and validity to the issue of the quality of value preferences. Even where there are both true reasons and no errors in the reasoning, you will not necessarily want to agree with the author. Before you make a decision, you need to consider carefully the major value conflicts and compare your value preferences to those of the writer. Once you have identified the writer's value preferences and your own, you have a basis for accepting or rejecting her conclusion on a rational level. It would make little sense to support conclusions or accept opinions that are supported by reasoning that is inconsistent with your personal value preferences. When you realize that an author's value preferences differ sharply from your own with respect to the controversy in question, you should be very cautious about accepting her reasoning. This chapter encourages you to use value preferences as a legitimate filter for deciding which opinions to accept.

A word of caution at the outset is needed. Just because a writer has value priorities that resemble yours does not mean that you should automatically agree with her conclusions. For example, you may both agree that the value of public health is greater than that of economic efficiency in the controversy concerning the severity of auto-emission control standards. You may not agree with her conclusion, however, because you may believe that her evidence has failed to show a clear public health risk or because you make different assumptions about how an auto-emission control program can best be implemented.

Thus, determining that a writer has value preferences similar to yours is only one step in critical reading. Each of the other critical questions must be answered satisfactorily before you can rationally make the author's conclusion yours.

Alternative Ways to Determine Your Value Preferences

If you are to match your value preferences with an author's, you must first identify value assumptions on both sides of the controversy. Chapter VI was devoted to helping you identify these assumptions. The next step is a decision about the confidence you should have in your own value preference.

Although we encouraged you to question conclusions that are based on values that you do not see as significant, we also want to urge you to examine your own values in the process. As you know, there are few universally accepted value assumptions. Maybe the ones you currently hold are simply the result of growing up in a particular family at a particular time in history. Since values play such a predominant role in influencing your behavior and beliefs, you owe it to yourself to think about changing your value assumptions. You cannot in any way *choose* your values unless you have thought seriously about the worth of alternative value assumptions.

By respecting value differences between yourself and others, you give yourself an opportunity to decide which set of values makes the most sense for you. You should ask yourself, Why is this set of values a good one? One way to answer this question is to examine the consequences of these values and to compare them to those of alternative values. Thinking about the consequences of different values permits you to explore the effects of valuing material success more than serenity, for example. It is fair to be dubious about conclusions when they are based on value assumptions you do not share. But as you are questioning these conclusions, spend a little time analyzing the strength of your commitment to the values that stimulated your reaction. Since values have such a powerful influence on your thinking, you must be very certain that you have chosen your values with care. A willingness to listen openly to those whose values differ from yours provides you with the opportunity to question your own value assumptions.

After you have reassured yourself that you indeed should have certain value preferences, there are several techniques you could use to justify these assumptions to yourself and others. It would be reasonable for someone to ask you where you got your value assumptions, suggesting that the quality of these assumptions depends on their source.

Several sources of value assumptions are repeatedly mentioned by those attempting to justify their value priorities:

1. Personal hunch
2. Authority
3. Tradition
4. Moral reasoning

These sources are so commonly used as the basis for value assumptions that we will discuss each one briefly.

When asked why they prefer patriotism to individualism in a particular controversy, many will simply say that it's obvious or common sense. Such an answer suggests that there is no basis for further questioning because the source is a personal hunch. To defend a value assumption based on a personal hunch, you can only assert that you have a strongly felt, unexplainable personal feeling, *period!*

Authority is another frequent source used to justify particular value assumptions. Asserting that one's value assumptions are derived from what one's family, priest, or political heroes believe avoids an explanation of why one has decided to let someone else be the source of these assumptions. The listener is asked to see the value assumption as appropriate solely because an authority approves.

A third way of justifying value assumptions is to base them on cultural or national traditions. The value assumption is deemed appropriate because the speaker has learned it from his community. Since these are the majority values, it is often assumed that they reflect some historical or collective wisdom. Many of those who use this justification would say. "Who am I to argue with the value assumptions of my community?"

The fourth common defense for value assumptions is *moral reasoning*. This view sees value preferences as legitimate to the extent that they are selected after rational argument and reflection. This source of values is based on an implied criticism of the other three sources. Thus, personal hunches, authority, and tradition may be starting points for justifying value assumptions; however, these sources must be examined rationally and critically. If they do not make sense as the source of some of our most fundamental beliefs, then the moral reasoning approach would reject the value assumptions that stem from them.

The first three sources of value preferences share a common problem. The person who accepts them as a proper source of justification tends not to ask himself whether the value assumption is reasonable. Instead, he obeys commands from sources beyond his control. He doesn't really choose value preferences; he accepts those chosen by others or those which pop immediately into his consciousness. Such an approach does not provide a technique for resolving value differences among people. There is no mechanism whereby one reassesses the worth of his value judgments in light of their consequences.

Moral Reasoning and Value Preferences

If you require that each of your value assumptions be justified by moral reasoning, you will always ask, Why is this my value preference in this situation? Is there some rational basis for believing that one value or set of values is any better than the other? Though you have already selected your value preferences, you should make a systematic attempt to justify their reasonableness.

How do you do this? The task is not simple. There are a number of ways to justify value priorities. We believe you will find the following suggestions helpful.

As explained in Chapter VI, the basic way to provide reasons for particular value assumptions is to examine the consequences or probable outcomes consistent with the value assumptions. What will be the societal effects of acting on the value preference you have chosen? Answering this question should form the basis for moral reasoning.

Let's look together at an illustration of the use of moral reasoning.

> We must legally prevent homosexuals from teaching in the public schools. The scientific evidence that homosexual conduct is caused neither by genes nor by birth defects is overwhelming. The homosexual chooses to be sexually attracted to members of the same sex. Consequently, we should not pity and protect homosexuals, since they knowingly choose to endure the social judgments that are applied to them.
>
> Since homosexuality is learned, we all must be concerned about who is teaching our children. If a child has an openly homosexual teacher, will not the child be attracted to the homosexual life? We do not want our children to see homosexuals in such positions, since they might get the impression that homosexuality is a harmless option.
>
> There is an abundance of evidence that homosexuals recruit young people. Many homosexual periodicals have numerous want ads, complete with nude poses, from homosexuals soliciting partners. Most of these ads are aimed at children under 18. School teachers who are homosexuals are in an ideal position to recruit pupils into a life of homosexuality.

The structure of this argument can be summarized in the following manner:

CONCLUSION: *Homosexuals should not be permitted to teach in public schools.*

REASONS: 1. *We should not protect homosexuals because they knowingly choose to endure the negative social judgments applied to them.*
2. *Since homosexuality is learned, children might be tempted to adopt this lifestyle if it is presented as a harmless option.*
3. *Homosexuals recruit young people, and teachers are in an ideal position to engage in such recruitment.*

For purposes of the illustration, overlook the sloppy evidence, reasoning errors, and questionable assumptions in the passage. *Imagine* that all three reasons are strong.

A value preference that stands out as very significant to the author of the passage is that tradition is a more important value than toleration of alternative lifestyles. He does not argue that homosexuality is bad; rather his arguments assume that homosexuality, like polio, is something which all people should be protected from. Why? He probably argues in this way because heterosexuality has *traditionally* been the only acceptable lifestyle. Suppose, again for purposes of the illustration, that you agree with the value preference of the author. Then ask yourself what consequences you would expect from acting on this value assumption. You should be able to identify both positive and negative consequences.

On the positive side, a society that emphasizes tradition tends to be more stable. Basic behavior and definitions of right and wrong persist for long periods of time. Those reared in such a society are not faced with choosing from among different roles. They know what is expected of them and can focus their energies on fulfilling that role. Tradition reflects a respect for one's ancestors and elders. Traditions develop over long periods of time, so they are the product not of whim and spontaneity but of historical evolution.

On the negative side, those devoted to tradition tend to resist change. Many useful ideas will probably be rejected in the interests of preserving traditional modes of thinking and behaving. Those who value tradition very highly may engage in harsh forms of repression as a means of restricting change. Such repression endangers the safety and material well-being of those attempting to change traditions.

Next, let's look at the probable consequences of valuing toleration of alternative lifestyles very strongly. Toleration of alternative lifestyles offers encouragement to other people to develop habits and skills in all the variety of ways possible to the human imagination. A world in which such a value is emphasized would be more diverse and would tend to permit human potential the broadest possible fulfillment. Less time and energy would be spent trying to restrict the behavior of others. At the same time, toleration of alternative lifestyles as a value does not lead to a clearly defined set of social and cultural standards. Many people are troubled when faced with numerous choices about what is appropriate or good. Such people need rules as a framework for their lives, and toleration of alternative lifestyles often leads to a rejection of such rules.

What we have attempted to do is suggest some consequences that tend to occur when either tradition or toleration of alternative lifestyles is a dominant value. You should next ask *why* these particular consequences are good or bad. Then you may question the basis for the answer, and so on. At some point you will simply decide that you have traced the rationale for the value preference back as far as your time allows. This chapter, by asking you to justify your value preferences by identifying some of the consequences of acting on them, provides a method for looking at least one level beyond an instinctual acceptance of certain values.

When you anticipate the consequences of acting upon particular value preferences, there are two problems that you will want to recognize. Initially, you need to be able to demonstrate that the predicted consequences are highly probable. It makes little sense to focus on outcomes that are only remotely possible. In the preceding illustration, for example, several historical examples in which groups had been persecuted by those preserving traditions would make it more convincing that valuing tradition very highly may indeed lead to repression. Only those consequences that are very likely should strongly affect your selection of value assumptions. Second, even if you show that the consequences are highly probable, you must present arguments that demonstrate the goodness or badness of particular consequences. If one effect of acting upon your value assumption is the closing of many small businesses, you will still have to form a reasonable argument for why that effect is good or bad as you justify your value assumption. When you can show that the consequences of your value assumption are both highly probable and better than those flowing from alternative value assumptions, *then* you have engaged in responsible moral reasoning.

XV

Judging the Worth
of Opinions:
Making Tentative Decisions

You now have many of the tools you need to form reasoned personal opinions. The techniques you have learned can save you from sloppy thinking and from being unduly influenced by the thinking of others, but they cannot provide you with a set of indisputably correct answers to the complex dilemmas you will face. They *will* enable you to avoid being a sponge in reacting to other people's attempts to persuade you and will thus permit you to make decisions that are the right ones for you and your value system.

Inappropriateness of Certainty

You can never be sure that your opinions are correct. You can have more confidence in carefully reasoned opinions than you can in other kinds, but the complexity of most important questions requires you to form conclusions before you can be absolutely certain that you are right. Even when we *know* we cannot be wrong, there is some shred of information we have not yet considered or some important implication of our conclusion that we have failed to analyze. Most of us want to be certain that our opinions are accurate, but the limitations of our intellects and the complexities of human dilemmas work together to frustrate this search for certainty. Thus, you should not define a good decision or conclusion as an absolutely correct one, but rather as the best you can achieve given your present limitations.

Making Tentative Personal Decisions

After you have asked the right questions, you are ready to form your reasoned conclusions. You should begin by reminding yourself what the controversy is. In arriving at a decision, it is of utmost importance to do the following:

1. List those reasons that you were least able to criticize.
2. List alternative inferences.
3. Make explicit the personal value preferences and definitions of key ambiguous terms that are relevant to this particular controversy.

Once you have done this, it is time to make your decision.

As you reach decisions, be sure to pay attention to each of these three products of your critical thinking. It may be tempting to use only value assumptions or only evidence in your rush to make a decision. To remind yourself of the need to consider precise definitions, reasons, and value assumptions, ask before each decision, "Under what conditions would I change my mind?" For example, you might oppose seat-belt legislation simply because you prefer individualism to public safety. By asking yourself what would have to be true for you to change your mind, you will be forced to consider how many injuries and fatalities would cause you to change your decision.

Your decision will be tentative in most cases. Answers to your questions will not be enough to provide you with certain conclusions. Whatever you decide, you should realize that a different conclusion might be more reasonable if only you knew more about each controversy. But making reasoned tentative decisions is rewarding for those who have gone through the necessary steps.

In many cases, because the reasoning you have encountered may be so weak or so abbreviated, the best tentative decision will be no decision. You will want to wait until you can find the relevant information elsewhere. In such cases, asking the right questions will have been useful to you because you will have been cautious enough not to be led to a premature judgment by a weak argument.

While you may frequently choose to put off making a decision, many issues will require conclusions right away, although it might take a decade to gather all the relevant information. Many of the debates discussed in this book require answers *now*. We need to help schizophrenics *now*. If foods are causing cancer, we need to act *now*. Decisions about building nuclear plants need to be made *now*. Thus, even though you would like to be sure before you form an opinion, you will often have to make a decision without delay.

When Has a Writer Done His Job?

One final precautionary note. If you consistently ask the right questions, we will be surprised if you do not have a tendency to judge virtually everything you read as a bad argument, or as a weak argument. Why? Because all of the arguments related to the kinds of issues we have been talking about will be flawed *in some respect*—if only because the writer does not have sufficient space to present his point of view thoroughly. You will find that it is much easier to find a flaw in someone else's reasoning than to construct your own reasoned arguments. Thus, keep in mind limitations as you judge the writer of a magazine article, a letter to the editor, an editorial, or a textbook. No position will be perfect, but some will be better than others. What you decide to call a well-reasoned article will be up to you. You now have the tools to judge the weak from the strong. But we suggest that you do not demand perfection and that you keep the writer's purpose in mind.

Look for the *best* argument you can expect, given the writer's purpose and the complexity of the issue.

Putting it All Together

You are now ready to form your opinions. To help you put it all together, the next and final chapter presents a checklist of critical thinking steps and takes you through one long example of critical thinking in action. This is an illustration of what you should now be able to do—engage in a process that culminates in reasoned opinions. We suggest that you keep the checklist handy as you practice applying the skills you have learned.

XVI

Practice
and
Review

You now know what questions you need to ask in order to be a critical reader. You have gone through many chapters and have become acquainted with many critical questions. In this chapter, we put it all together for you. We will begin by again listing the critical questions. This checklist should serve as a handy guide for you until the questions become second nature. When you encounter articles, lectures, debates, textbooks, commercials, or any other materials relating to an issue that is important to you, you will find it useful to go through the checklist and check off each question as you ask it.

Next, we provide an essay that demonstrates the usefulness of the critical questions for clear writing. This essay, on the subject of licensing parents, is a model of writing that communicates precisely what its author intends. You can use it to guide the format of the essays *you* write. As you read the essay, you will notice how the author has anticipated the critical questions that readers using the filter model will be asking.

In the final section, we apply the critical questions in critically evaluating one position on a contemporary controversy. The major purpose of this discussion is to provide an example of a coherent application of *all* the critical reading steps.

We suggest that you follow the discussion with several goals in mind. You can treat it as a check on your understanding of previous chapters. Would you have asked the same questions? Would you have formed similar answers? Do you feel better able to judge the worth of someone's reasoning? After all, that is the whole purpose of asking the right questions.

Checklist for Critical Reading

CRITICAL QUESTIONS:

1. What are the issue and the conclusion?
2. What are the reasons?

3. What words or phrases are ambiguous?
4. What are the value conflicts and assumptions?
5. What are the definitional and descriptive assumptions?
6. Are the samples representative and the measurements valid?
7. Are there flaws in the statistical reasoning?
8. Are there alternative causal explanations?
9. Are there any errors in reasoning?
10. What significant information is omitted?
11. What alternative conclusions are consistent with the strong reasons?
12. What are your value preferences in this controversy?

Applying the Critical Questions to Your Writing

Before writing an essay, you must first think carefully about several matters. Certainly you must consider the nature of your audience, as well as any time or space limitations. You will want to vary the sophistication of your language depending upon whether your readers are experts in the field about which you are writing or members of the general public. The type and extent of evidence to include will depend on audience and space considerations.

In addition, you will need a writing strategy that will provide your readers with the message you intend. In planning your strategy, you can benefit from an awareness of the critical questions that readers might apply to your essay. You can achieve clarity by critically reviewing your writing from the point of view of a critical reader asking these or similar questions about your essay.

The following essay is a model of clarity by a careful writer. Within his space limitations, he demonstrates an awareness of the critical questions. As you will see, the essay reflects his expectation that certain filters or criteria will be applied to his reasoning.

Licensing Parents

HUGH LaFOLLETTE[1]

In this essay I shall argue that the state should require all parents to be licensed. My main goal is to demonstrate that the licensing of parents is theoretically desirable, though I shall also argue that a workable and just licensing program actually could be established.

---

[1]Hugh LaFollette, "Licensing Parents," *Philosophy and Public Affairs*, Vol. 9, No. 2 (Winter 1980). Copyright © 1980 by Princeton University Press. Excerpt pp. 182–189 reprinted with permission of Princeton University Press.

My strategy is simple. After developing the basic rationale for the licensing of parents, I shall consider several objections to the proposal and argue that these objections fail to undermine it. I shall then isolate some striking similarities between this licensing program and our present policies on the adoption of children. If we retain these adoption policies—as we surely should—then, I argue, a general licensing program should also be established. Finally, I shall briefly suggest that the reason many people object to licensing is that they think parents, particularly biological parents, own or have natural sovereignty over their children.

Regulating Potentially Harmful Activities

Our society normally regulates a certain range of activities; it is illegal to perform these activities unless one has received prior permission to do so. We require automobile operators to have licenses. We forbid people from practicing medicine, law, pharmacy, or psychiatry unless they have satisfied certain licensing requirements.

Society's decision to regulate just these activities is not ad hoc. The decision to restrict admission to certain vocations and to forbid some people from driving is based on an eminently plausible, though not often explicitly formulated, rationale. We require drivers to be licensed because driving an auto is an activity which is potentially harmful to others, safe performance of the activity requires a certain competence, and we have a moderately reliable procedure for determining that competence. The potential harm is obvious: Incompetent drivers can and do maim and kill people. The best way we have of limiting this harm without sacrificing the benefits of automobile travel is to require that all drivers demonstrate at least minimal competence. We likewise license doctors, lawyers, and psychologists because they perform activities which can harm others. Obviously they must be proficient if they are to perform these activities properly, and we have moderately reliable procedures for determining proficiency.[2] Imagine a world in which everyone could legally drive a car, in which everyone could legally perform surgery, prescribe medications, dispense drugs, or offer legal advice. Such a world would hardly be desirable.

Consequently, any activity that is potentially harmful to others and requires certain demonstrated competence for its safe performance, is subject to regulation—that is, it is theoretically desirable that we regulate it. If we also have a reliable procedure for determining whether some-

[2]"When practice of a profession or calling requires special knowledge or skill and intimately affects public health, morals, order or safety, or general welfare, legislature may prescribe reasonable qualifications for persons desiring to pursue such professions or calling and require them to demonstrate possession of such qualifications by examination on subjects with which such profession or calling has to deal as a condition precedent to right to follow that profession or calling." 50 SE 2nd 735 (1949). Also see 199 US 306, 318 (1905) and 123 US 623, 661 (1887).

one has the requisite competence, then the action is not only subject to regulation but ought, all things considered, to be regulated.

It is particularly significant that we license these hazardous activities, even though denying a license to someone can severely inconvenience and even harm that person. Furthermore, available competency tests are not 100 percent accurate. Denying someone a driver's license in our society, for example, would inconvenience that person acutely. In effect that person would be prohibited from working, shopping, or visiting in places reachable only by car. Similarly, people denied vocational licenses are inconvenienced, even devastated. We have all heard of individuals who had the "life-long dream" of becoming physicians or lawyers, yet were denied that dream. However, the realization that some people are disappointed or inconvenienced does not diminish our conviction that we must regulate occupations or activities that are potentially dangerous to others. Innocent people must be protected even if it means that others cannot pursue activities they deem highly desirable.

Furthermore, we maintain licensing procedures even though our competency tests are sometimes inaccurate. Some people competent to perform the licensed activity (for example, driving a car) will be unable to demonstrate competence (they freeze up on the driver's test). Others may be incompetent, yet pass the test (they are lucky that certain aspects of competence—for example, the sense of responsibility—are not tested). We recognize clearly—or should recognize clearly—that no test will pick out all and only competent drivers, physicians, lawyers, and so on. Mistakes are inevitable. This does not mean we should forget that innocent people may be harmed by faulty regulatory procedures. In fact, if the procedures are sufficiently faulty, we should cease regulating that activity entirely until more reliable tests are available. I only want to emphasize here that tests need not be perfect. Where moderately reliable tests are available, licensing procedures should be used to protect innocent people from incompetents.[3]

These general criteria for regulatory licensing can certainly be applied to parents. First, parenting is an activity potentially very harmful to children. The potential for harm is apparent: Each year more than half a million children are physically abused or neglected by their parents.[4]

---

[3]What counts as a moderately reliable test for these purposes will vary from circumstance to circumstance. For example, if the activity could cause a relatively small amount of harm, yet regulating that activity would place extensive constraints on people regulated, then any tests should be extremely accurate. On the other hand, if the activity could be exceedingly harmful but the constraints on the regulated person are minor, then the test can be considerably less reliable.

[4]The statistics on the incidence of child abuse vary. Probably the most recent detailed study (Saad Nagi, *Child Maltreatment in the United States*, Columbia University Press, 1977) suggests that between 400,000 and 1,000,000 children are abused or neglected each year. Other experts claim the incidence is considerably higher.

Many millions more are psychologically abused or neglected—not given love, respect, or a sense of self-worth. The results of this maltreatment are obvious. Abused children bear the physical and psychological scars of maltreatment throughout their lives. Far too often they turn to crime.[5] They are far more likely than others to abuse their own children.[6] Even if these maltreated children never harm anyone, they will probably never be well-adjusted, happy adults. Therefore, parenting clearly satisfies the first criterion of activities subject to regulation.

The second criterion is also incontestably satisfied. A parent must be competent if he is to avoid harming his children; even greater competence is required if he is to do the "job" well. But not everyone has this minimal competence. Many people lack the knowledge needed to rear children adequately. Many others lack the requisite energy, temperament, or stability. Therefore, child-rearing manifestly satisfies both criteria of activities subject to regulation. In fact, I dare say that parenting is a paradigm of such activities since the potential for harm is so great (both in the extent of harm any one person can suffer and in the number of people potentially harmed) and the need for competence is so evident. Consequently, there is good reason to believe that all parents should be licensed. The only ways to avoid this conclusion are to deny the need for licensing *any* potentially harmful activity; to deny that I have identified the standard criteria of activities which should be regulated; to deny that parenting satisfies the standard criteria; to show that even though parenting satisfies the standard criteria there are special reasons why licensing parents is not theoretically desirable; or to show that there is no reliable and just procedure for implementing this program.

While developing my argument for licensing I have already identified the standard criteria for activities that should be regulated, and I have shown that they can properly be applied to parenting. One could deny the legitimacy of regulation by licensing, but in doing so one would condemn not only the regulation of parenting, but also the regulation

[5]According to the National Committee for the Prevention of Child Abuse, more than 80 percent of incarcerated criminals were, as children, abused by their parents. In addition, a study in the *Journal of the American Medical Association* 168, no. 3: 1755–1758, reported that first-degree murderers from middle-class homes and who have "no history of addiction to drugs, alcoholism, organic disease of the brain, or epilepsy" were frequently found to have been subject to "remorseless physical brutality at the hands of the parents."

[6]"A review of the literature points out that abusive parents were raised in the same style that they have recreated in the pattern of rearing children. . . . An individual who was raised by parents who used physical force to train their children and who grew up in a violent household has had as a role model the use of force and violence as a means of family problem solving." R. J. Gelles, "Child Abuse as Psychopathology—a Sociological Critique and Reformulation," *American Journal of Orthopsychiatry* 43, no. 4 (1973): 618–19.

of drivers, physicians, druggists, and doctors. Furthermore, regulation of hazardous activities appears to be a fundamental task of any stable society.

. . . In the next section I shall see if there are any special reasons why licensing parents is not theoretically desirable . . .

Theoretical Objections to Licensing

Licensing is unacceptable, someone might say, since people have a right to have children, just as they have rights to free speech and free religious expression. They do not need a license to speak freely or to worship as they wish. Why? Because they have a right to engage in these activities. Similarly, since people have a right to have children, any attempt to license parents would be unjust.

This is an important objection since many people find it plausible, if not self-evident. However, it is not as convincing as it appears. The specific rights appealed to in this analogy are not without limitations. Both slander and human sacrifice are prohibited by law; both could result from the unrestricted exercise of freedom of speech and freedom of religion. Thus, even if people have these rights, they may sometimes be limited in order to protect innocent people. Consequently, even if people had a right to have children, that right might also be limited in order to protect innocent people, in this case children. Secondly, the phrase "right to have children" is ambiguous; hence, it is important to isolate its most plausible meaning in this context. Two possible interpretations are not credible and can be dismissed summarily. It is implausible to claim either that infertile people have rights to be *given* children or that people have rights to intentionally create children biologically without incurring any subsequent responsibility to them.

A third interpretation, however, is more plausible, particularly when coupled with observations about the degree of intrusion into one's life that the licensing scheme represents. On this interpretation people have a right to rear children if they make good-faith efforts to rear procreated children the best way they see fit. One might defend this claim on the ground that licensing would require too much intrusion into the lives of sincere applicants.

Undoubtedly one should be wary of unnecessary governmental intervention into individuals' lives. In this case, though, the intrusion would not often be substantial, and when it is, it would be warranted. Those granted licenses would face merely minor intervention; only those denied licenses would encounter marked intrusion. This encroachment, however, is a necessary side-effect of licensing parents—just as it is for automobile and vocational licensing. In addition, as I shall argue in more detail later, the degree of intrusion arising from a general licensing program would be no more than, and probably less than, the present (and presumably justifiable) encroachment into the lives of people who apply to adopt children. Furthermore, since some people hold unacceptable views about what is best for children (they think children should be abused regularly), people do not automatically have rights to rear children just because they will rear them in a way they deem appropriate.[7]

Consequently, we come to a somewhat weaker interpretation of this right claim: A person has a right to rear children if he meets certain minimal standards of child rearing. Parents must not abuse or neglect their children and must also provide for the basic needs of the children. This claim of right is certainly more credible than the previously canvassed alternatives, though some people might still reject this claim in situations where exercise of the right would lead to negative consequences, for example, to overpopulation. More to the point, though, this conditional right is compatible with licensing. On this interpretation one has a right to have children only if one is not going to abuse or neglect them. Of course the very purpose of licensing is just to determine whether people *are* going to abuse or neglect their children. If the determination is made that someone will maltreat children, then that person is subject to the limitations of the right to have children and can legitimately be denied a parenting license.

In fact, this conditional way of formulating the right to have children provides a model for formulating all alleged rights to engage in hazardous activities. Consider, for example, the right to drive a car. People do not have an unconditional right to drive, although they do have a right to drive if they are competent. Similarly, people do not have an unconditional right to practice medicine; they have a right only if they are demonstrably competent. Hence, denying a driver's or physician's license to someone who has not demonstrated the requisite competence does not deny that person's rights. Likewise, on this model, denying a parenting license to someone who is not competent does not violate that person's rights.

Of course someone might object that the right is conditional on actually being a person who will abuse or neglect children, whereas my proposal only picks out those we can reasonably predict will abuse children. Hence, this conditional right *would* be incompatible with licensing.

---

[7]Some people might question if any parents actually believe they should beat their children. However, that does appear to be the sincere view of many abusing parents. See, for example, case descriptions in *A Silent Tragedy* by Peter and Judith DeCourcy (Sherman Oaks, CA.: Alfred Publishing Co., 1973).

There are two ways to interpret this objection and it is important to distinguish these divergent formulations. First, the objection could be a way of questioning our ability to predict reasonably and accurately whether people would maltreat their own children. This is an important practical objection, but I will defer discussion of it until the next section. Second, this objection could be a way of expressing doubt about the moral propriety of the prior restraint licensing requires. A parental licensing program would deny licenses to applicants judged to be incompetent even though they had never maltreated any children. This practice would be in tension with our normal skepticism about the propriety of prior restraint.

Despite this healthy skepticism, we do sometimes use prior restraint. In extreme circumstances we may hospitalize or imprison people judged insane, even though they are not legally guilty of any crime, simply because we predict they are likely to harm others. More typically, though, prior restraint is used only if the restriction is not terribly onerous and the restricted activity is one which could lead easily to serious harm. Most types of licensing (for example, those for doctors, drivers, and druggists) fall into this latter category. They require prior restraint to prevent serious harm, and generally the restraint is minor—though it is important to remember that some individuals will find it oppressive. The same is true of parental licensing. The purpose of licensing is to prevent serious harm to children. Moreover, the prior restraint required by licensing would not be terribly onerous for many people. Certainly the restraint would be far less extensive than the presumably justifiable prior restraint of, say, insane criminas. Criminals preventively detained and mentally ill people forceably hospitalized are denied most basic liberties, while those denied parental licenses would be denied only that one specific opportunity. They could still vote, work for political candidates, speak on controversial topics, and so on. Doubtless some individuals would find the restraint onerous. But when compared to other types of restraint currently practiced, and when judged in light of the severity of harm maltreated children suffer, the restraint appears *relatively* minor.

Furthermore, we could make certain, as we do with most licensing programs, that individuals denied licenses are given the opportunity to reapply easily and repeatedly for a license. Thus, many people correctly denied licenses (because they are incompetent) would choose (perhaps it would be provided) to take counseling or therapy to improve their chances of passing the next test. On the other hand, most of those mistakenly denied licenses would probably be able to demonstrate in a later test that they would be competent parents.

Consequently, even though one needs to be wary of prior restraint, if the potential for harm is great and the restraint is minor relative to the harm we are trying to prevent—as it would be with parental licensing—then such restraint is justified. This objection, like all the theoretical objections reviewed, has failed.

A particular strength of LaFollette's essay is that it is remarkably free of ambiguity, logical fallacies, and misused statistics. For instance, take another look at the section where he addresses the right to have children. He explicitly recognizes the potential ambiguity of the term by stating three alternative meanings. He then explains why he believes that the third interpretation is the most reasonable. Finally, he demonstrates the consistency between that interpretation and the conclusion he has suggested.

In addition, LaFollette demonstrates an awareness of the potential problems with reasoning by analogy. He does this by listing the important characteristics shared by other regulated activities and showing how parenting possesses these characteristics. He thus anticipates the reader's critical question about the quality of the analogy.

A final strength of LaFollette's writing is his recognition of the role played by assumptions in his reasoning. His anticipation of the objections his opponents would raise demonstrates the importance of identifying the assumptions lurking below the surface in your own reasoning. For example, he recognizes that his opponents will point out the harm that would result when someone is denied a license to have a child. LaFollette's argument is based in part on the assumption that the social benefit of licensing parents exceeds the damage to the needs of prospective parents. By being aware of that assumption and defending it, LaFollette provides us with a more complete version of the argument he has in mind.

Naturally enough, LaFollette's essay has weaknesses. For instance, although the statistics he provides to show the extent and effect of child abuse are from highly respected sources, he does not explain how the data were generated. Thus, we cannot have complete confidence in their accuracy. However, the provision of some data from reputable sources is far better than providing the reader with no evidence. In addition, the essay fails to discuss a central issue—the measure that would be used to determine the competence of a prospective parent. Despite these problems, however, LaFollette's writing is unusually clear and should be useful as a model for your own writing.

Asking the Right Questions: A Comprehensive Example

We first present a passage that summarizes one position with respect to the desirability of using racial characteristics as a basis for admitting students to graduate and professional schools. This section is followed by a lengthy critical discussion based on all twelve critical questions.

(1) Most professional schools have many more applicants for admission than the schools can admit. (2) Since access to education that will result in graduates becoming doctors, dentists, or lawyers is so valuable an opportunity, this access should not be decided by reference to the racial characteristics of applicants. (3) Yet many nonwhites argue for admissions policies that reflect "affirmative action." (4) Affirmative action is a euphemism for making admissions decisions on the basis of race. (5) Those for whom racial equality has been requested are now trying to be more equal than white applicants to professional schools. (6) If admissions and hiring decisions are illegal when they exclude nonwhites from fair consideration, then they should be illegal when they favor these same nonwhites.

(7) Affirmative action admissions policies for professional schools are disruptive, unnecessary, and even dangerous. (8) If one desires racial harmony, as I do, then affirmative action policies that unfairly aid nonwhites will be disruptive of our hopes. (9) Whites who are denied access, as well as their sympathizers, will probably be quite negative in their future attitudes toward nonwhites. (10) Affirmative action reminds us of our race and the fact that other racial groups are advancing at our expense. (11) If the objective that affirmative action is attempting to achieve is more nonwhite doctors, lawyers, and dentists, then a more acceptable option would be the creation of more professional schools.

(12) Those who support admissions policies based on affirmative action should be very careful. (13) If the goal of these policies is to bring representation in professions up to a level consistent with the minority's representation in the general population, then shouldn't the same reasoning be applied to other occupations? (14) Since there are a disproportionate number of nonwhites on professional sports teams, wouldn't it be a natural extension of affirmative action admissions policies to require coaches to reserve a certain number of team positions for white players?

(15) Affirmative action admissions policies are highly discriminatory. (16) How do admissions committees decide which minorities to discriminate in favor of? (17) Surely many other groups besides nonwhites are treated unfairly in our society. (18) In all seriousness, why shouldn't women and poor, fat, ugly, or dirty people be given preference for admissions, since no one can deny that they have been victims of prior discrimination? (19) In fairness we should either grant special admission privileges to all past victims of injustice or else we should continue the current admissions policies based on merit.

(20) Nonwhites who are not qualified simply should not be granted scarce training slots in professional schools. (21) The United States Post-Secondary Testing Center has conclusively demonstrated that the average nonwhite applicant is less qualified than is his white counterpart. (22) Yet we all know that under the guise of affirmative action, this inequity is encouraged. (23) For instance, a recent survey of law schools estimated that 80 percent of black law students admitted in 1976 would not have been admitted in open competition with whites. (24) Twenty percent of white law students, but only 1 percent of black and 4 percent of Chicano applicants, have undergraduate averages above 3.25 and LSAT scores above 600. (25) Thus, we are undercutting the quality of our professions by admitting relatively unqualified applicants.

What follows should serve as a comprehensive model of the product of critical reading. It proceeds in a step-by-step sequence based on the twelve critical questions. Though it will not offer a final conclusion, it will provide a reasonable basis on which *you* can make a decision.

[WHAT ARE THE ISSUE AND CONCLUSION?]

The passage denies the desirability of affirmative action admissions policies in the professional schools which train the nation's doctors, lawyers, engineers, and administrators. It is clearly opposed to the creation and continuation of special admissions policies for minority applicants. This conclusion is a response to the issue, Are affirmative action admissions policies for professional schools desirable?

[WHAT ARE THE REASONS?]

Let's paraphrase the reasons that lead to the conclusion that affirmative action admissions policies in professional schools are undesirable.

1. *If racial discrimination is illegal, discrimination against whites is also illegal. (sentences 2–6)*
2. *By highlighting racial characteristics, affirmative action admissions policies create greater hostility between whites and nonwhites. (sentences 7–10)*
3. *An alternative method for creating more nonwhite professionals is the sponsorship of more professional schools. (sentence 11)*
4. *The absurdity of attempting to assure that the proportion of nonwhites in each occupation is equal to the proportion of nonwhites in the workforce can be seen if one will admit that competence in particular occupations may not be distributed identically to the distribution of racial characteristics in the population. (sentences 13–14)*
5. *Class and sex are as important as race in determining social inequity. Thus, a focus on race perpetuates inequity while pretending to limit it. (sentences 15–19)*

6. *Nonwhites admitted to professional schools by affirmative action admissions policies are frequently relatively unqualified. Admitting unqualified applicants eventually reduces the quality of professional services. (sentences 20–25)*

[WHAT WORDS OR PHRASES ARE AMBIGUOUS?]

In the arguments against affirmative action admissions, we look first for possible ambiguity that might weaken the reasoning presented, keeping in mind that we should be focusing on the author's major reasons. An important ambiguity pervades the entire argument concerning the desirability of affirmative action admissions policies. What precisely are affirmative action admissions policies? Notice how one's reaction to their desirability would be affected by the choice of either of the following alternative definitions:

a. *Active efforts to seek talented minority students in high school and then provide them with special training so they can eventually meet existing professional school admissions standards.*

b. *Encouragement of a racial quota which the admissions office is pledged to meet. Failure to meet the quota must be explained fully to the public.*

The first definition would find many more supporters because these kinds of affirmative action policies are more consistent with the competitive and individualistic values that predominate in our culture. That definition requires all applicants to eventually meet the same standards prior to admission. Yet we cannot tell from the passage what the author means by "affirmative action policies."

[WHAT ARE THE VALUE CONFLICTS AND ASSUMPTIONS?]

One value conflict that has a strong impact on this entire debate is that between (A) *equality of condition*, defined in this instance as minorities receiving a proportional number of admission slots in graduate and professional schools, and (B) *individualism*. Those who attack affirmative action admissions policies tend to prefer individualism to equality of condition. They assume that it's up to each individual to earn the right to a position in graduate or professional school without any help from the government. This value assumption links the set of reasons to the conclusion. Equality of condition would result in the type of proportional representation condemned explicitly in the fourth reason. A preference for equality of condition over individualism might cause one to reject the author's conclusion while granting both the truth of each of the reasons and the absence of any errors in reasoning. In such an instance, a strong preference for equality of condition over individualism might lead to the conclusion that affirmative action admissions policies are needed.

Other value conflicts that affect the author's reasoning can be derived from a closer look at individual reasons. The second reason reflects a value preference for social harmony over racial equality. The claim that affirmative action admissions policies will cause hostility between blacks and whites is based on the fear that whatever social harmony now exists would be disrupted by immediate movement toward racial equality. The sixth reason is based on the value assumption that excellence is a more important value than equality of condition. The alleged negative effect of affirmative action admissions policies is that future professionals will be less competent. The author is apparently less concerned about assuring proportional representation of minorities among professionals than he is about the level of skill exhibited by graduates of professional schools.

[WHAT ARE THE DEFINITIONAL AND DESCRIPTIVE ASSUMPTIONS?]

One definitional assumption made by the author involves the use of *applicant quality*. In sentences 20 through 25, it is alleged that nonwhites admitted under affirmative action guidelines are often relatively unqualified. Yet the evidence that is presented is all based on a particular definition of applicant quality—namely, school performance records and their correlates. A broader definition of applicant quality that incorporated such applicant characteristics as verbal communication skills, willingness to empathize, or breadth of appreciation for the impact of life-style of clients on their behavior, might result in a very different attitude toward the worth of affirmative action admissions policies.

At least two descriptive assumptions play a key role in shaping the attack on these policies. The first reason assumes that the past history of the treatment of racial groups should not be a consideration in determining the fairness of hiring policies. The author fails to recognize that rewarding certain representatives of a racial group may be the most effective strategy for compensating those who have been prior victims of racial discrimination. The author fails to consider the historical context in which affirmative action is occurring; thus he perceives hiring and admissions decisions based to any degree on racial considerations as universally repugnant.

The second reason assumes that white reaction to such admissions policies will be molded by the predictably negative attitude of rejected white applicants. This assumption is questionable, since the white-dominated legislative bodies which have enacted civil rights and equal opportunity statutes apparently have sensed a growing commitment on the part of white voters to affirmative action policies. The author asks us to believe that this support for affirmative action will wither as soon as rejected white applicants become visible. Perhaps he is right, but the assumption he makes is only hypothetical.

[ARE THE SAMPLES REPRESENTATIVE AND THE MEASUREMENTS VALID?]

Some of the evidence used in making the case against affirmative action admissions policies is also flawed. Notice in particular the evidence used for the sixth reason. Sentences 23 and 24 refer to a survey of law schools from which the authors infer nonwhite candidates are less qualified than white applicants for admission. However, we are told very little about how the survey was conducted. How many schools were surveyed? How representative were the schools? How did they define *quality*? For example, it would be helpful to know whether the schools surveyed had identical definitions of applicant quality. If their definitions are divergent, use of a common definition in a later study might lead to very different inferences.

[ARE THERE FLAWS IN THE STATISTICAL REASONING?]

Sentence 24 provides us with data which appear to indicate the relatively poor quality of nonwhite law students. A couple of possible problems in this data should prevent us from immediately inferring that the quality of law schools and the legal profession would be diminished by affirmative action policies. First, he is comparing very different groups. The grade point averages and LSAT scores of white law *students* are compared to those of nonwhite *applicants* to law school students. Surely, those admitted would have higher average scores than would the total set of applicants. The author apparently set up the comparison of scores so that it would be most supportive of his conclusion. Finally, the study cited may mean nothing more than that nonwhite applicants are less capable *students* than are white applicants. It does not necessarily follow that affirmative action admissions would result in less capable *lawyers*.

[ARE THERE ALTERNATIVE CAUSAL EXPLANATIONS?]

Sentences 8 through 10 attempt to attribute increasing racial hostility to affirmative action policies. These sentences do not present a very convincing causal explanation. They certainly don't reflect a controlled study determining the effect of these policies on incidence and severity of racial hostility. Sentence 9 is especially weak because it overlooks the positive effect on whites' attitudes toward blacks of seeing successful black professionals in their midst.

[ARE THERE ANY ERRORS IN REASONING?]

The third reason offers a proposed alternative method for increasing the number of nonwhite professionals. The alternative is in some sense a diversion. Many of the arguments for affirmative action admissions policies are based on a concern for the *relative* number of nonwhite professionals, rather than the *absolute* number. Therefore, sentence 11 is not an argument against attempts to increase the *proportion* of nonwhite professionals.

The fourth reason also has a logical problem associated with it. It is not a convincing argument to a claim that such proportions should not be imposed on the professions because they are ignored in other key occupations such as in sports. This reason employs a questionable analogy. In sports there are clear performance criteria. Coaches and general managers will want players on their teams who can run faster, score more often, or serve more effectively. If a particular racial group has these skills disproportionately, they will predominate in a particular sport. However, there are no similarly clear criteria for what makes a competent lawyer, doctor, or engineer. Thus, the argument in the fourth reason that a criterion that would be unfair in sports is equally unfair in determining who gets into graduate school is not convincing.

In at least one more respect the analogy in the fourth reason is flawed. The skills required to become a successful law or medical student are acquired in our educational system. There is no similarly strong link between schools and the development of sports skills. It is probable that there has been significant historical discrimination against racial minorities in our educational system and no similar discrimination in the process whereby sports skills are developed. Therefore, there is a basis for providing affirmative action help to racial minorities when they seek admission to graduate and professional schools; no corresponding basis is available to support the use of affirmative action in athletics.

Even if the analogy were a strong one, a supporter of affirmative action admissions policies could reasonably respond by noting that the existence of one misallocation of job slots does not provide a defense for continued misallocations in other occupations. Such supporters might see the professional schools as but the first battleground in a general struggle against occupational discrimination defined in terms of a smaller proportion of desirable job slots than would be held if the percentage of job slots by racial grouping equaled the percentage of that racial category in the workforce. A similar response could be made in answer to the fifth reason: Yes, we should compensate all groups victimized by previous discrimination; but we must start somewhere, and racial discrimination is as significant a focus for our initial efforts as would be any other form of past inequity.

Two more blatant reasoning errors are committed in sentences 19 and 22. Sentence 19 commits an either-or error. The author gives the reader only two choices—either all victims of past injustice should be aided by affirmative action or no victim should be aided. That false dilemma makes little sense. Many alternative actions are possible. Helping a few who have been mistreated would make a start toward a fairer society. The demonstration effect of such an expression might encourage further efforts to compensate for past injustices. Alternatively, there may be many effective ways to help certain groups that do not require affirmative action. Some victims of past injustice may need affirmative action and others may need a different social commitment. Sentence 19 does not permit that flexibility.

Sentence 22 attempts to persuade through the use of the phrase "we all know that." But the author does not tell us *why* we should agree with most people that the subsequent generalization is accurate.

[WHAT SIGNIFICANT INFORMATION IS OMITTED?]

One highly significant piece of information that would be useful to know in evaluating the first 25 sentences is the extent to which school performance predicts success as a professional. In the medical field, postoperative juries can assess the need for and quality of surgery. However, in most professional areas the definition of competence is vague. Consequently, in the absence of any consistent data relating professional competence to school performance, the common measures of applicant quality (on which so much of the argument against affirmative action admissions policies is based) are suspect. If someone could demonstrate a strong relationship between school and work performance by professionals, the arguments in the first 25 sentences would be more potent.

[WHAT ALTERNATIVE CONCLUSIONS ARE CONSISTENT WITH THE STRONG REASONS?]

Let's first list the strong reasons—that is, those we were least able to criticize. Next we will identify any alternative conclusions consistent with these reasons.

1. *If racial discrimination is illegal, discrimination against whites is also illegal.*

2. *Class and sex are as important as race in determining social inequity. Thus, a focus on race perpetuates inequity while pretending to limit it.*

Remember that we are looking for conclusions other than the one provided by the author that are reasonable inferences on the basis of the strongest reasons we could find in the passage.

One alternative conclusion is actually hinted at in the passage—work to make discrimination against blacks and whites illegal. Until the legality of such policies is determined definitively, there will continue to be widely divergent admissions policies by professional schools. An equally reasonable conclusion that could be inferred from the two strong reasons is that affirmative action admissions policies based on sex and class should be encouraged. Notice that this inference is quite different from the one reached by those who sugggested the arguments, but it is just as consistent with their reasons.

[WHAT ARE YOUR VALUE PREFERENCES IN THIS CONTROVERSY?]

We are not going to state a value preference of our own. We will suggest some of the possible consequences associated with placing a heavy value on either individualism or equality of condition. From studying these consequences, you can select your personal value preference with respect to the desirability of affirmative action admissions policies at graduate and professional schools.

Individualism usually leads to a wide range of achievement. In a society in which each person is encouraged to achieve as much as possible without any help from anyone else, it is highly probable that levels of achievement will vary greatly. Some members of society will be very rich, famous, and skilled; others will be poor and forgotten. Individualism tends to create a society in which people are very possessive and property-conscious. Those emphasizing individualism believe that an individual typically gets what he deserves; consequently, the comfortable *deserve* their comfort and the miserable have earned their misery. Such beliefs provide support for widely unequal distributions of property and income. The rewards for success and the penalties for failure are generally great when individualism is emphasized.

Equality of condition tends to create a loss of incentive. The necessity for struggle is much less if there is a social assurance that equal results will eventually be provided regardless of performance. In such a society those who wish to distinguish themselves from others by earning lots of money often express their unwillingness to work hard when such striving offers them no clear reward. This value is conducive to social stability, however, because it stimulates few of the tensions among classes that are often associated with great inequality. Those who would have otherwise lived lives of poverty often feel part of a cooperative community when equality of condition is a prevailing social value.

Our critical reading is completed and the personal part of decision making remains. Our critical discussion responds to only *some* of the facets of the controversy over affirmative action admissions policies. You may want to focus on other parts of the argument. Ultimately, *you* must decide which of the inferences to support.

Critical reading can take you only so far. The final step is yours. You can feel relatively confident after following our checklist that you have asked the right questions about the arguments and that you are finally ready to form a reasoned opinion of your own.

Index